Legends from Papua New Guinea

BOOK 2

collected by **Donald S. Stokes**

retold by **Barbara Ker Wilson**

OXFORD
UNIVERSITY PRESS

253 Normanby Road, South Melbourne, Victoria 3205, Australia

Oxford University Press is a department of the University of Oxford.
It furthers the University's objective of excellence in research, scholarship, and education by publishing worldwide in

Oxford New York
Auckland Cape Town Dar es Salaam Hong Kong Karachi Kuala Lumpur Madrid Melbourne Mexico City Nairobi New Delhi Shanghai Taipei Toronto

With offices in

Argentina Austria Brazil Chile Czech Republic France Greece Guatemala Hungary Italy Japan Poland Portugal Singapore South Korea Switzerland Thailand Turkey Ukraine Vietnam

First published 1978 by Hodder and Stoughton (Australia) Pty Limited, 2 Apollo Place, Lane Cove NSW 2066 in association with Hodder and Stoughton Children's Books, Sevenoaks, Kent
Reprinted 2002, 2005, 2015(D)

ISBN 0 19 554077 8.

Text and cover design by Kirstin Lowe
Map by Joseph Lucia
Cover illustration by Gigs Wena
Printed in Australia by Ligare Pty Ltd

CONTENTS

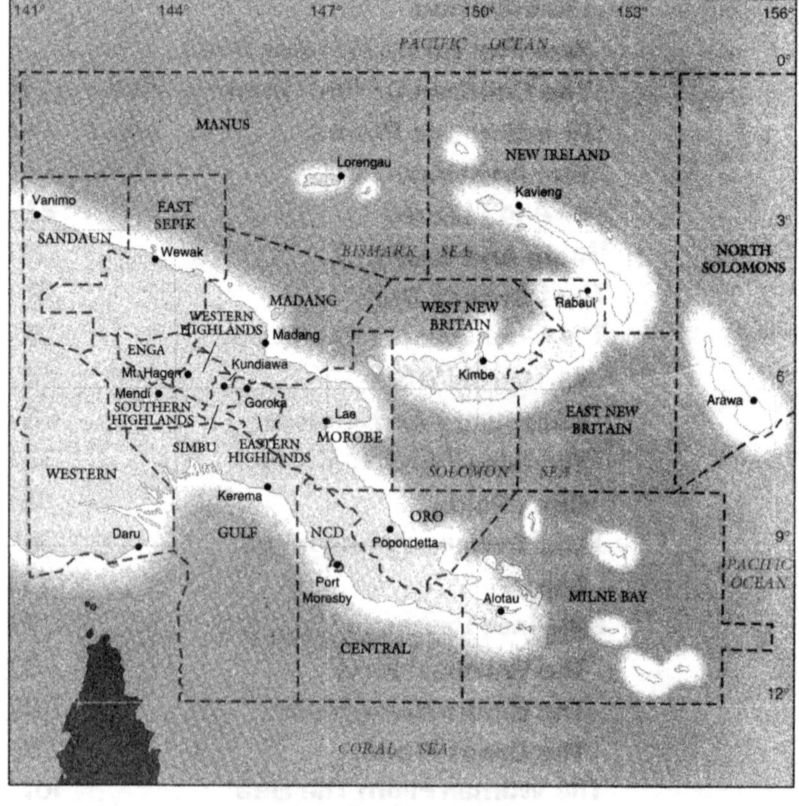

Papua New Guinea

INTRODUCTION

The stories in ***Legends from Papua New Guinea: Book Two***, originally published in 1978 under the title *The Turtle and the Island*, have stood the test of time well. They have given readers both inside and outside Papua New Guinea insights into the rich cultures of the country. Above all, they have demonstrated that scientific explanations and descriptions do not constitute the only valid way of viewing the world—something all too often overlooked in this age of technology. Some of the stories, for example, give explanations about the origin of fire, the formation of islands, the emergence of new plants, and the birth of volcanoes. They are enlightening because they link human beings understandably and inseparably to their environment.

Other stories present moral and ethical codes in equally poignant and memorable ways. *Papaya* shows that beauty is more than skin-deep. *Sun And Sago* is about disobedience and its consequences. *The Children Of The Omokoy Tribe* teaches the necessity to invite to traditional functions, all the people who should be invited. *Galo And Vasiri* emphasises the importance of showing love and respect towards family members. And the *Ant And Lizard* illustrates the destructive force that jealousy plays in a relationship.

During my years in Papua New Guinea, I was deeply impressed by the young students I met, first at the University of Papua New Guinea, and, later, at the Institute (now University) of Technology, in Lae. They were fully conscious of their status as role models and as possible future leaders of the nation. They experienced life between two worlds, coping with the new, while remaining intent upon maintaining their ties to their traditional heritage. As well as knowing several languages besides their own tok ples, they had internalised the oral literature that had, for generations, defined their physical and social environments.

The stories in ***Legends from Papua New Guinea, Book Two*** were written initially by students at the University of Technology in 1970 and 1971 as contributions to a student yearbook called *Nexus*. Many of these stories had never been translated into English before. Seven years later, in 1978, a representative selection of stories from *Nexus* was published in The Turtle and The Island, retold by Barbara Ker Wilson. The origins of the stories were carefully noted on the maps on the end papers of the book. In addition, the biographical details of the students who contributed the stories were provided in a special section just after the introduction.

Today, these former students are adults, in positions of responsibility not only as citizens of the nation, but also as older members in families of their own. They have every reason to take pride in the cultural diversity that the stories exhibit. Their stories can be legitimately viewed as part of the legacy given by past generations to the nation's future.

Just as the topographical landscapes of Papua New Guinea are constantly changing because of natural forces such as earthquakes and volcanic eruptions, the September 1994 volcanic eruptions in Rabaul, for example; so also, are the cultural landscapes of the country changing.

Languages and cultures are changing, some are merging with neighbouring ones, and virtually all are being influenced by those of the outside world. In this process, it is inevitable that there are going to be gains and losses.

It is hoped that the young people of today will see the stories in ***Legends from Papua New Guinea, Book Two*** as memorable examples of the country's immense cultural treasures, which they themselves can help to collect and preserve, just as the contributors of the stories in this collection have done.

Donald S. Stokes
Australia
1996

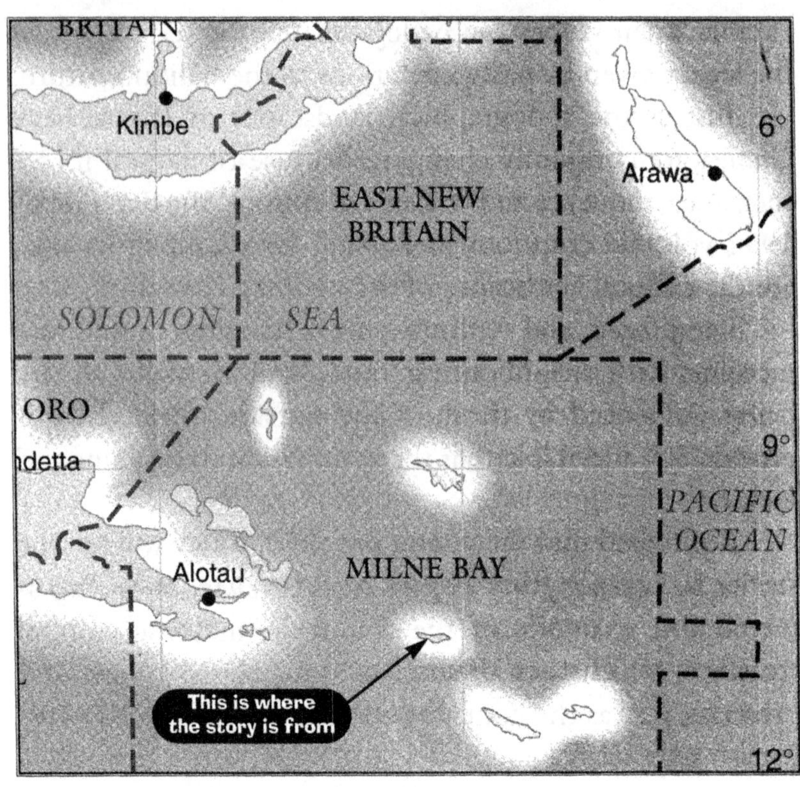

How The Turtle Got Her Shell **was contributed by Amo Mark. Amo comes from Liak village, on Misima Island in the Milne Bay Province.**

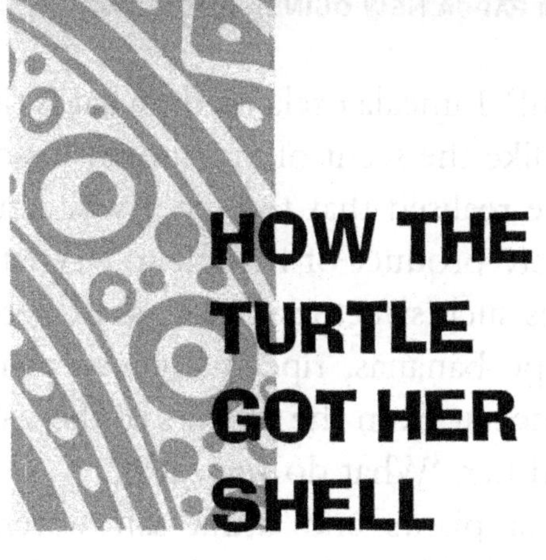

HOW THE TURTLE GOT HER SHELL

Once upon a time, Tameala the turtle and Bebebi the butterfly were close friends. Tameala looked very different in that long-ago time, for she did not have a shell. Bebebi was a huge butterfly with bright orange, black and green patterned wings. They made a strange contrast, these two friends. The turtle was a slow, plodding creature, while the butterfly was always flitting from place to place. However, in the heat of the day they enjoyed sitting on the soft sand under the shade of a giant banyan tree, gossiping about things that did not matter. When other people criticised them and scolded them for being lazy, they laughed and took no notice.

One day, while they were sitting in their favourite place, Tameala decided to move a big rock nearby. She pushed and strained at it, and as she did so, some wind escaped from her body. Bebebi immediately flew into the air to get away from the smell. Luckily, the breeze dispersed it quickly. As the butterfly settled again, he planned to pay back Tameala for that, and presently he felt his inside move and was able to do so.

'Geh-yah!' Tameala exclaimed, 'what is that sweet fragrance? It is like the scent of manibolu blossom!'

Then she realised that the scent was actually coming from the waste product of her friend. 'What do you eat, that produces such sweetness?' she asked Bebebi.

'I eat ripe bananas, ripe mangoes—plenty of fruits, and I drink nectar from the flowers of the wild bush,' the butterfly told her. 'What do *you* eat?'

'I eat sea plants and drink salt water,' the turtle replied. 'I should like to know what your food tastes like. Why don't we both fetch some of our food here and then we can try each other's and see whether we like it?'

Bebebi thought this a good idea, so they both went off to gather food. At sunset they returned and put their food on the ground beneath the banyan tree.

'Eat everything I have brought and tell me which food you like best,' Bebebi told Tameala. 'Meanwhile, I will try your food.'

The turtle picked up a banana, peeled it delicately, and gobbled it up. 'Delicious!' she pronounced, as clearly as she could, for her mouth was crammed full.

The butterfly picked up a small piece of sea plant and began to chew it. 'Very pleasant,' he decided. 'A sharp taste, but a nice change after all the sweet foods I am used to.'

Tameala, who was inclined to be greedy, quickly tasted some mango and drank some flower nectar from a shell. 'Now I have tasted all the food you brought,' she told Bebebi. 'I like the banana the best. Could you show me where bananas grow?'

'Of course,' Bebebi replied. 'Follow me.'

He led the turtle to the gardens close by where many

banana trees grew. Bunches of many-fingered ripe bananas hung down from the tree stems. The two friends ate and ate until their bellies could hold no more. As they left the gardens, Bebebi warned Tameala that the trees belonged to the villagers, who planted them and cared for them. They were very valuable. 'Anyone who steals from the trees is put to death,' he told her.

But Tameala, the greedy one, did not heed Bebebi's words. The very next evening she came to the gardens again, and as she was stuffing her fifth banana into her mouth, three angry villagers jumped out and caught her. So many bananas had been missing from the trees that morning that they had lain in wait to see if the thief would return.

'Tomorrow we will feast on turtle flesh!' the village chief proclaimed. 'Today, let every man, woman and child go out to collect more food and firewood for the feast.'

All the villagers did as they were told, except for an old, blind woman who was left to guard the turtle and make sure it did not escape. As soon as the last person had disappeared from sight, Tameala spoke to the old woman. 'As you can see, this rope that binds my arms is cutting into my flesh and bruising it. It really would be much better if you untied my bonds, so that when I am killed for the feast, my flesh will be unmarked and you will be able to eat every part of me.'

The old woman was not very clever. She thought the turtle's advice sounded sensible, and without thinking twice, she slashed the rope that held Tameala captive. The turtle at once picked up a piece of wood from the ground and held it out to the old woman. 'Take hold of my arm,' the turtle said. 'Don't loosen your grip or I might escape!'

Then Tameala set off for the seashore. How she longed to immerse herself in the cool sea after standing in the hot sun for so long! But she knew that because she went so slowly with her plodding gait, she might not reach the sea before the villagers returned and discovered she had escaped. She picked up a beautifully grained wooden ceremonial bowl as she went, and carried it on her back as she crawled off to the shore.

Soon the villagers returned bearing wood for the cooking fires and food for the feast. They were astonished to see the old, blind woman sitting beside the stake in the middle of the village, holding a piece of of wood.

'Where is the turtle?' they screamed.

'Surely you can see that I am holding on to her arm,' the old woman replied. 'I untied her bonds so that her flesh would not be bruised.'

'You stupid old woman!' shouted the chief. 'Don't you realise that what you are gripping so tightly is nothing but a piece of wood? The turtle has deceived you and escaped!'

Then, one of the villagers saw the track of the turtle, leading towards the sea. All the men got their spears ready and set out in pursuit.

Tameala had just reached the water's edge when her pursuers came running on to the beach. They flung their spears, but the turtle was protected by the ceremonial bowl she had put on her back, and she swam into the sea unharmed. When she was a safe distance away she looked back at the villagers and called out to them: 'Return to your village and eat the pieces of firewood you gathered to roast my flesh!'

Then she dived into the water and swam and swam until she came to a small, uninhabited island called Bunola. She lived there for many, many years, for a turtle's life is a long, long one, and she produced many young turtles. The ceremonial bowl on her back had protected her so well that she never removed it. Strange to say, the young turtles born to her each had a little bowl on their backs as well; and ever since that day all turtles have had shells. If you scrub a turtle's shell thoroughly, you can still see the beautiful grain of the original bowl that Tameala picked up in the village. Today, the little island of Bunola, not far from Misima Island, in the Louisade Archipelago, is still uninhabited by man, but there are hundreds of Tameala's descendants there. It is sometimes known as the isle of the turtles.

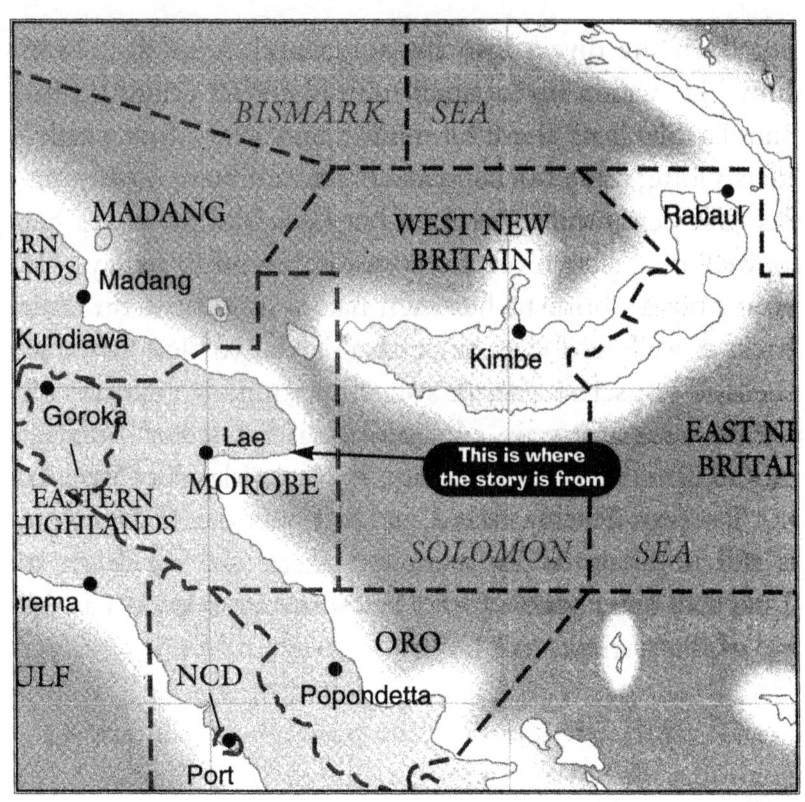

The Children Of The Omokoy Tribe **was contributed by Bindim Salomo. Bindim comes from Nasingalatu village, in the Morobe Province.**

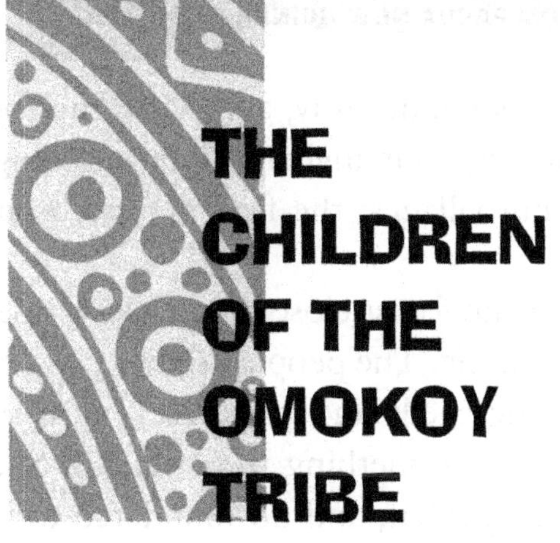

THE CHILDREN OF THE OMOKOY TRIBE

Once, long ago, there was a certain tribe known as the Omokoy, or Dog People tribe. The Omokoys inhabited the region of Finschhafen, at the end of the Huon Peninsula. Their life was peaceful and prosperous: no warlike neighbours attacked them, no droughts spoiled their crops. Their old people were wise and respected, their young men brave and strong, their women handsome and contented. Above all, these happy people loved their children, who ran about playing and laughing all day long. Fish teemed in the sea and there were plenty of wallabies, possums and pigs in the bush. The cooking fires never lacked for meat, and the women brought ample supplies of yams, sweet potatoes, mangoes and pawpaws from the gardens. Not only did these fortunate villagers have enough food for themselves, they were able to invite neighbouring villages to feasts and sing-sings; they loved to make music and dance.

The chief of the village was called Yokomo, which means 'the happy leader'. One day, Yokomo decided it was time he invited his neighbours to join the Omokoy people for another feast. He told his villagers to begin the preparations straight away, and while the food was being cooked, he sent out invitations by messenger to all the neighbouring villages: the feast was to be held that very night.

Now in the forest close by, an old woman, who was a witch, lived alone. The people used to go to her when they wanted magic spells and potions to cure sickness, or to help them gain something they wanted. She grew magic plants in her garden, and no one dared to venture inside it.

Yokomo the happy chief always used to invite the witch to every feast he gave, but today he forgot to tell his messenger to invite her. The witch heard the villagers preparing for the feast; in the distance she heard them practising the flute and beating the kundu drums—and she waited in vain for Yokomo's invitation. It did not come.

'I will pay back Yokomo for this!' she muttered angrily. 'Yokomo, the happy chief, will need a new name by the time his feast is over!'

When darkness came, the whole of Yokomo's village was alive with music and singing. Mouth-watering aromas came from the meat roasting on the cooking fires; baskets were piled high with ripe mangoes and pawpaw and the sound of laughter was in the air. It was the custom of the Omokoy people always to invite their beloved children to join them in their feasting, but that night a strange thing happened. Just as the celebration was beginning, the witch disguised herself as one of the village women, and came among the people with a special drink she had prepared from the leaves of the magic irina tree. When Yokomo and his people sipped this drink, their heads became muddled and they forgot to call their children to come to eat with them; in fact, they forgot about their children altogether as they went on singing and laughing, dancing and feasting.

Left alone in the biggest house in the village, the children waited and waited for Yokomo the chief to call them to the feast. One of the children was so disappointed and angry that he suggested they should all run away into the forest and stay there for a while. 'That will give Yokomo and our parents a good fright,' he said. 'It will serve them right for their selfishness. They won't forget to invite us next time!'

The other children thought this a good plan. 'But how shall we escape without anyone seeing us?' they asked each other.

The witch overheard what they were planning, and saw her chance to punish the village still further. Stealthily, she crept up to the children and told them that she knew an easy way for them to leave the village. She made each child fetch a large bilum, a string bag, and then she showed them how to step inside these bags. No sooner was each child inside, than the witch uttered powerful magic and in an instant all the bilums were turned into wings, a pair for each child.

'Fly away! Fly far away!' she cried. 'You will never live here with your parents again!'

Then, in a close company, all the children of the Omokoys rose up and flew into the forest, while the witch returned to her home.

The next day, Yokomo and his villagers recovered from the effects of the witch's magic drink, came to their senses and realised that all their children had gone.

Whereupon they set up a great wailing. Sorrow had come to that village, which had known only happiness for so long.

The children, meanwhile, had flown so far that they were exhausted. They rested in the trees all that day, using their bilum-wings to hang themselves up in the branches. The next night they flew through the darkness back to their village, and took their revenge on their forgetful parents by going into the gardens and taking all the ripe fruit—bananas, mangoes, pawpaws—that they could find. The next night and the next, and every night for ever afterwards, the children of the Omokoy tribe continued to raid the fruit trees in the gardens—for the witch had turned them into the creatures that men call flying foxes. All through the centuries they have caused great damage to the fruit trees, and it is very difficult to hunt them, for they always hide themselves during the day, hanging upside-down from the branches of trees in the forest. The tree they haunt the most is the irina. These flying foxes, descended from the Omokoy Tribe, the Dog People of long ago, have faces like a dog's, and their wings are veined with a network of blood vessels like the interlacings of a string bag.

FIVE STRANGE PLANTS

This is a tale told by the Tolai people of New Britain. It tells of a long-ago time when the world was young, so young that many of the plants which grow today were not yet known.

In a cave on a mountainside lived a fierce, wicked old man called ToKonokonomlor. *To* is the first part of any Tolai name; *Konokonom* means 'to swallow', and *lor* means 'the head of a man', ToKonokonomlor was a cannibal who used to prey on the village that lay below the mountain. Although he was old and short of stature, he was as strong as a crocodile; and although he had a face as wrinkled as a flying fox's, he had won for himself four wives. Their names were IaBuai, IaVudu, IaLama and IaKado.

ToKonokonomlor used to attack the villagers at night. He would track down anyone he saw walking alone, man or woman, on the outskirts of the village and spear them. Then, he would take his victim back to his cave, cut off the head and tell his wives to cook the rest of the body for him to eat.

At last the time came when the villagers could no longer endure ToKonokonomlor's evil habit. The men

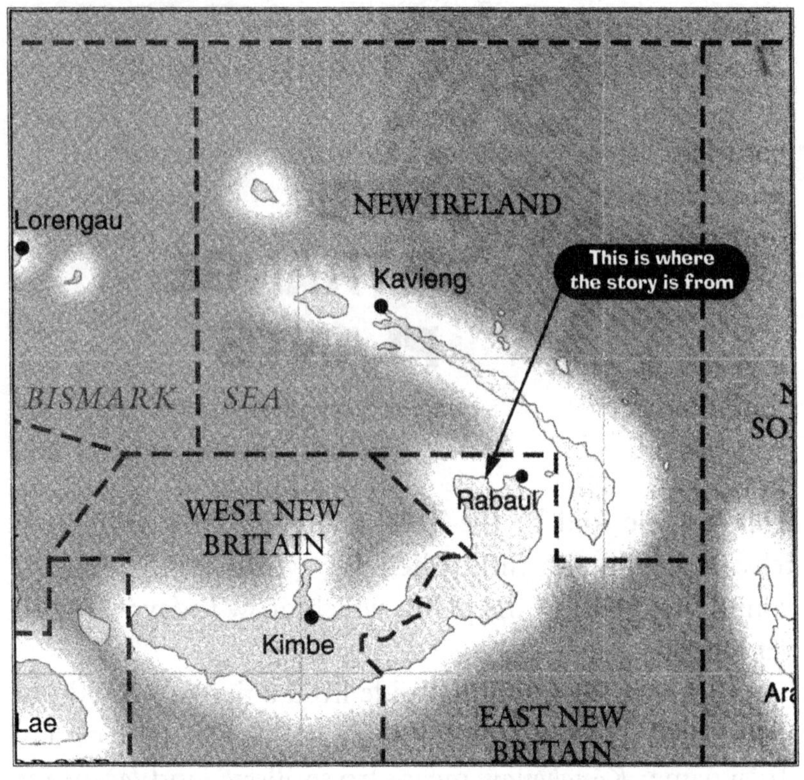

Five Strange Plants **was contributed by Bobo Akuila. Bobo comes from Kanavi village in the East New Britain Province. He attended Lae Technical College, before going on to the University of Technology, Lae, to study civil engineering.**

gathered together in the meeting-house to discuss how they might get rid of the old man, who was as cunning as he was strong and ugly. They knew it would not be easy to overcome him.

Then a young man called ToGenau stood up and said, 'I have a plan to kill ToKonokonomlor.'

'What is it?' the other men asked him.

'I shall pretend I am a girl. I will wear a skirt and walk by myself as darkness is falling, singing and laughing to attract ToKonokonomlor's notice. Then, when you see him about to attack me, you must make a noise to divert his attention, and I will grab his spear and kill him.'

All the men decided this was a very clever plan. They were so pleased that they promised ToGenau that if all went well, he might have the most beautiful girl in the village as his wife, without having to think about the bride-price. They were all so confident that the plan would succeed, that they told their families to prepare for a big feast the next day, to celebrate ToKonokonomlor's death.

That night, the men waited silently in a big circle just outside the village, hidden in the shadows of the trees. Then, ToGenau came out of his hut, dressed like a girl, with a grass skirt worn low on his hips, a freshly-plucked wild hibiscus flower in his hair, and wearing a necklace of shells. He walked like a girl, swaying gently, and as he went into the shadowy trees, he sang softly in a high-pitched voice, and laughed as a young girl laughs.

Silently as a snail, ToKonokonomlor watched from the place where he stood hidden in the bush. He did not see the men encircling the village; he saw only the young girl with the flower in her hair who sang and laughed as she walked alone. ToKonokonomlor clutched his sharp spear. Stealthily he began to follow ToGenau, until he was within throwing distance. Suddenly a great noise of shouting and the beating of kundu drums broke the silence of the forest. Startled, ToKonokonomlor looked away from his victim; in that moment, the girl who was really ToGenau the young warrior dashed forward, seized the old cannibal's spear, overcame him, and dragged him back to the village.

There was great rejoicing that the cannibal who had terrorised the village for so long had at last been captured. The men cut off ToKonokonomlor's head, then set out for his cave in the mountainside to look for his four wives. They stood outside the entrance of the cave and called to each wife in turn.

'IaBuai!'

IaBuai emerged from the cave. Before she could look around to see who called, she was seized and her head was cut off.

'IaVudu!'

IaVudu came out, wondering who was there; and the same thing happened to her.

'IaLama!'

ToKonokonomlor's third wife appeared. Her end was as swift as the others'.

The fourth and youngest wife came last. And now all four wives were dead.

The men buried their bodies, then took their heads to show to the villagers. That night there was a big feast with a singsing that lasted until daybreak. In the morning, they were all exhausted with their joyful dancing.

While the others slept or lazed, ToGenau took the four heads of ToKonokonomlor's wives, as well as the head of the cannibal himself, and buried them in the hillside. As he was returning home, the sky clouded over and it grew dark. There was a fearful crash of thunder. ToGenau ran as fast as he could back to his hut in the village. He was surprised to find a young girl there, sheltering under the thatch that overhung the doorway. She was slim and comely, her skin gleaming, her eyes soft and welcoming as she saw ToGenau approach.

'Who are you? Did you fall from the sky when the thunder crashed?' he asked, amazed.

'No,' she answered, laughing. 'I belong to the village and I am to be your wife, according to the promise made in the meeting-house.'

ToGenau was overjoyed, for she was certainly the most sweet-natured as well as the most beautiful girl in the village. They became man and wife, and lived peacefully together.

But that is not the end of the story. After a while, ToGenau remembered how he had buried the heads of ToKonokonomlor and his four wives in the mountainside. He returned to that place: to his astonishment, five strange, unknown plants had sprung up. For their bravery in overcoming the wicked cannibal, the Tolai people were rewarded in this way: the head of IaBuai became the betel nut tree; the head of IaVudu became the banana plant; the head of IaLama became the coconut palm; and the head of IaKakao became the cacao tree. As for the head of ToKonokonomlor himself, that became the breadfruit tree.

The Tolai people soon discovered the uses of these five plants and learned how to grow them in their food gardens. And in time, these five crops provided them with great wealth, when in later years they began to trade.

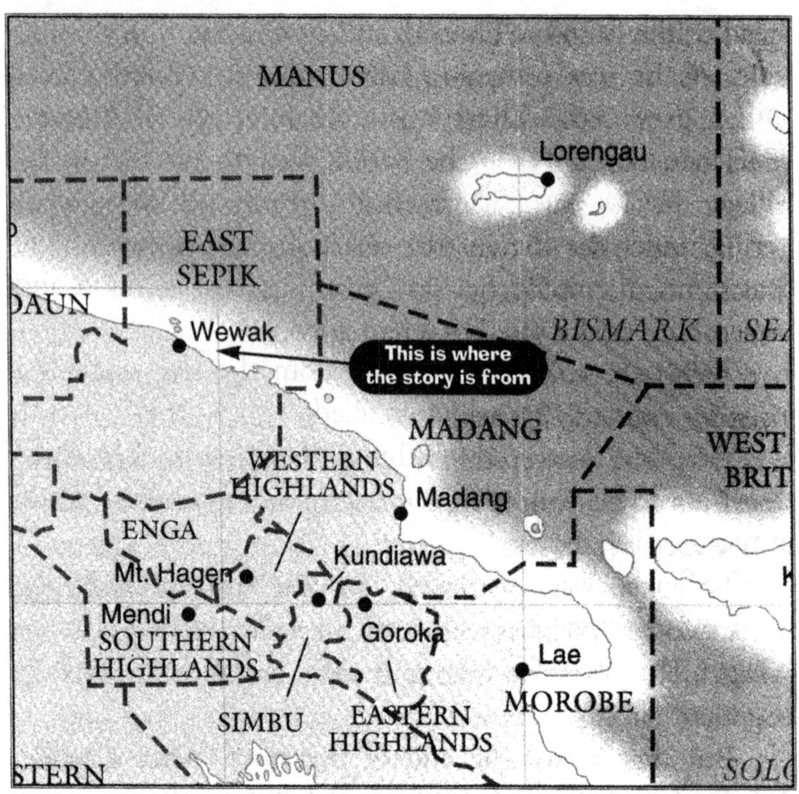

***Sun and Sago* was contributed by Adam Amod. Adam comes from Ali Island in the Sandaun Province. He attended St. Ignatius' High School, near Aitape, before going on to the University of Technology, Lae, to study civil engineering.**

SUN AND SAGO

In a far-distant time beyond the memory of the oldest man's great-grandfather, the Sun alone gave light to the earth. By day he sent down hot, fierce beams that lit up every part of the land. By night he felt so tired that he could produce only a feeble glimmer that left large areas of darkness. So the people who lived on the earth got into the habit of being awake during the hot, bright day and of sleeping through the cool, dark night. If the Sun had never grown tired, they might never have known sleep at all.

Along the great waterway which men now call the Sepik River, there lived a man called Keimbu, who had one wife, Belebile, a son, Yichye, and a daughter, Saiwe. They lived a peaceful life, hunting and gathering food. Twice a day, Belebile cooked their meals outside the hut Keimbu had built for his family. Each morning they ate sago. From time to time, Keimbu and Belebile would go out to the marshy places alongside the great river where the sago palms grew, small trees with thick trunks that stood in the water. The time to gather the sago was when the trees first produced their flower spikes, before the fruit developed. As soon as the flower spike appeared, Keimbu would cut down one of the trees, and then he and Belebile would take out all the starchy pith contained in the stems. Afterwards, Belebile would prepare the pith for cooking: she pounded it, kneaded it with water, strained it, washed it, and then it was ready to use—a soft, dry powder.

Yichye and Saiwe did not yet help to gather the sago, for they were still very young.

One day, after Belebile had prepared the evening meal, she decided to cook what was left of their store of sago. She knew there was just enough left for one more meal. Tomorrow, she and Keimbu must go out to gather more. When Belebile went to her little store of sago, however, she was astonished to find that it had turned into a large, shining, round object that glowed with a soft light.

'Aiee! This is strange and marvellous,' she cried; and she went to tell her husband and children of this discovery.

'Strange and marvellous!' echoed Keimbu. The children, too, exclaimed in amazement and delight.

Keimbu picked up the large glowing sphere and set it in the centre of the hut, where it gave out its soft light all round. Usually the family hurried over their eating each evening, but tonight, in the friendly glow of this strange lamp, they talked longer and enjoyed their meal more, and stayed awake much later.

Next day, Keimbu hid the glowing circle under the thatch of the roof, before he and Belebile set out to gather more sago from the palms beside the great river.

'Leave our treasure where I have hidden it,' Keimbu warned Yichye and Saiwe. 'Do not take it outside; an envious man might come by and steal it from us.'

Then he and Belebile went off to the great river.

The two children soon became bored inside the hut, and Yichye looked longingly up into the roof where they could see the strange object glowing through the thatch.

'Surely Father would not mind if we played with it inside the hut,' he said to his sister.

So they took down the shining ball—it was so large that it took both of them to lift it—and began to play with it, rolling it to each other across the floor of beaten earth. Suddenly Yichye rolled it too hard, so that it went right past Saiwe as she stood in the doorway of the hut, and rolled across the ground outside, halfway to the green forest beyond the clearing. The children ran after it, laughing. They had quite forgotten Keimbu's warning.

At that very moment the Sun was busy sending down his bright rays over the land. He was just beginning to feel weary because he was using up so much energy, yet he knew he might never rest. He happened to glance down at the exact spot where Yichye and Saiwe were chasing their new toy.

'What can that be?' the Sun wondered. 'It glows, it shines with a light which is like an echo of my own!' He peered down more closely. 'Now, if only I had that shining toy, I could set it in the sky beside me to help me in my work. Then, I could rest at night, while this strange toy shone instead of me, and I would no longer feel tired. For the truth is that if I continue to work night and day, as I do now, I shall become completely worn out.'

Well, the Sun wasted no more time; the next instant he slipped down to earth and stood beside the children, who flung up their arms to shield their eyes from his fierce glare, and shrank back from his burning presence.

'Come, children, let me have that shining ball you are playing with,' the Sun demanded; and as he spoke his hot breath scorched the leaves of the trees at the edge of the green forest.

'No—it belongs to Keimbu our father. We cannot let you have it!' Yichye was brave to protest so strongly, for he felt very afraid.

'Our father and our mother Belebile have gone to the great river to gather sago. They will be back soon and they will be very angry if you steal our treasure,' Saiwe said in a voice that quavered.

The Sun laughed; and now his scorching breath set fire to the grass, which began to crackle and blaze underfoot. 'I am not afraid of your father Keimbu, nor of your mother Belebile, nor of any man or woman on this earth. I am the mighty Sun! There is nothing and no one as strong and powerful as me!'

And now the Sun stooped down and took the glowing circle from the children. 'It is I who am angry,' he told Yichye and Saiwe, who stood and trembled while the grass fire licked their ankles. 'I shall punish you for daring to disobey me. I am going to take you far, far away from your parents to a place beyond their reach. Yet they will be able to see you when they look up to the sky at night; and you will be able to see them if you look down upon the earth.' He tucked the two unhappy children under one arm, and with the glowing ball held firmly in his other hand, he leapt back into the sky. Then, he placed Yichye and Saiwe on top of the circle, and set it forever high, high in the sky, so that it might help him with his work by night. And in time men called that strange, round, glowing object the Moon.

For the rest of their time on earth, the sorrowful Keimbu and Belebile could only gaze at their two children from a far distance, when the Moon shone by night. The two black spots they could see on the surface of the Moon: those were Yichye and Saiwe, taking their never-ending punishment from the Sun.

All these things happened a long time ago, and the lives of Keimbu and Belebile have long since passed away; but today, if anyone gazes at the Moon, they can still see those two black spots on its surface.

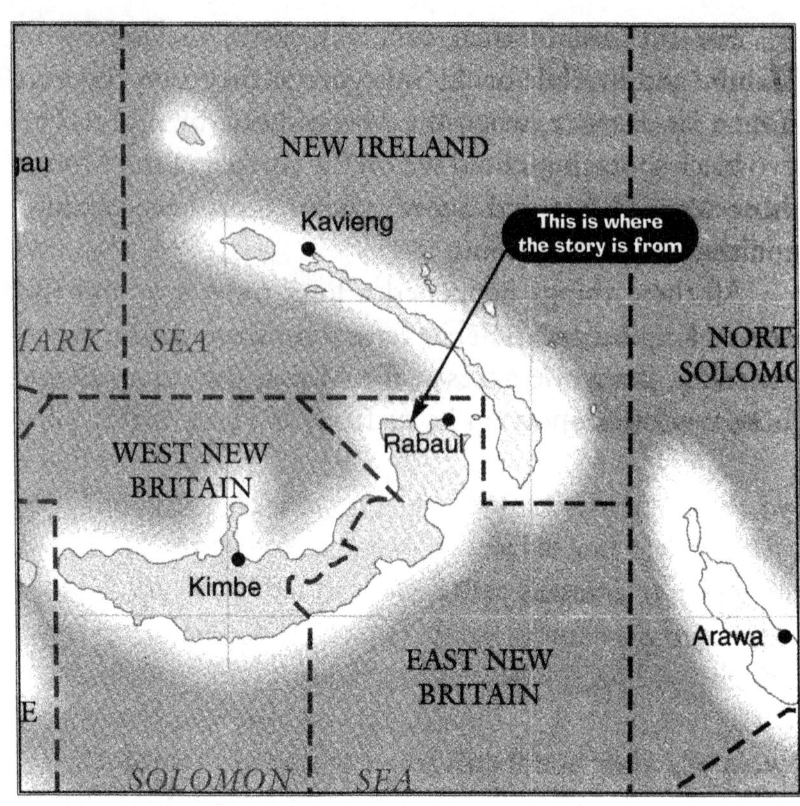

Ant And Lizard **was contributed by John Paivu. John comes from Kuraip village in the East New Britain Province.**

ANT AND LIZARD

If you cast your glance upon the ground as you walk along, you will never see an ant and a lizard playing together, however long you look and however far you walk. This has been so ever since the great battle which once took place between the ants and the lizards—a battle greater than any tribal clash before or since. Yet there was a long-ago time, when the ant and the lizard were firm friends. They used to live side by side, sharing their food and all their possessions. They would go hunting together, swim together in the sea, sing and dance and feast together, and smile and laugh as they joked with each other.

The trouble between them began one year when food became scarce. This did not trouble the ant, since he was so small that he needed very little to eat, but it was a more serious matter for the big fellow, the hungry lizard. One morning, the two friends went off hunting together as usual, equipped with spears and nets. When they reached their hunting ground, the lizard stopped beneath a mango tree and said: 'Ant, you go and look for a pig. I'll be waiting up on a branch of this tree. Drive the pig here, and I'll jump down on him and finish him off.'

So the ant went looking for a pig—and he found one: a big, fat pig. He began to drive it towards the mango tree, stinging it in the rear-quarters to hurry it along. As soon as the pig came beneath the mango tree, the lizard jumped out and fell on to the pig's broad back. The pig was angry and shook its body this way and that, and the next instant the lizard landed amidst the thick kunai grass.

The ant, who had watched this happen, ran round to his friend as he lay in the grass. He laughed at the lizard and made fun of him with many witty words. 'See how the brave hunter has fallen amid the spears!' he said—for the kunai grass was sharp and prickly. 'Never mind, Lizard, we'll try again. This time *you* go looking for the pig, and I'll wait in the mango tree.'

So the lizard went away, and after a long time he finally tracked down the pig and began to chase it towards the mango tree. As soon as the ant saw the pig beneath him, he jumped on to its head and quickly killed it by stinging and stinging its eyes.

The ant then sang a song of triumph, but the lizard stayed silent and sulky; he was angry because the ant had mocked him when he lay in the kunai grass, and was jealous of his friend's success.

They took the pig home and began to *mumu* it: they placed it in their oven, a shallow pit dug in the earth, and covered it with hot stones. Then, the lizard suggested that while they waited for the pig to roast, they should go for a swim. The ant agreed, and they went down to the sea together and got into their canoe. When they had paddled a long way from the shore, the lizard suggested that each of them in turn should try to swim down to the bottom of the sea, and, if they succeeded, bring up a quantity of sand to prove it. The ant thought this was a good way of passing the time, and he tried first, but he could not reach the bottom. Indeed, he tried more than once, because each time he surfaced, the lizard smacked him with the canoe paddle and sent him down again.

'See the brave diver, how he will not give up his attempt to reach the bottom of the sea!' mocked the lizard.

At last the ant climbed back into the canoe, and now it was the turn of the lizard. He jumped into the sea, and immediately swam as fast as he could under water, heading for home. Once ashore, he ran back to the mumu and began to eat the roasted pig, tearing greedily at its tender, succulent flesh.

The ant, sitting alone in the canoe, became suspicious of the lizard's long absence. 'Something tells me that our friendship is coming to an end,' he thought sadly; and then he picked up the paddle and made his way home. There, beside the mumu sat the lizard, still eating the pig-meat.

'Lizard,' the ant said sorrowfully, 'it is clear that after this day we can no longer go hunting or play together. But let us eat the remainder of this pig together as friends for the last time.'

Soon they had eaten every scrap and their bellies were full. Then the ant said: 'Today marks the end of our friendship, and as a sign that this is so, you must blow your tavur shell, and I will blow mine, to call our relatives to this place. When we are ready, we will fight until one of us wins the battle.'

So the lizard sounded his tavur: a big, cone-shaped shell with a hole in its side; and every lizard alive, black, white, huge, small, long-tailed, stumpy-tailed, every single kind, crawled out from the bush and waited for the battle to begin.

The ant sounded his tavur, and immediately thousands of ants—black, white, red, large, tiny, in fact ants of every description—swarmed to that place, and they too waited for the signal to join battle.

One—two—three: the battle began! It was long and fierce; it was waged on the ground, up in the trees, down in the bush, over the house roofs, everywhere. The ants and the lizards tore into each other with fury, using every fighting skill they knew. At one moment, it seemed the lizards were winning, but then the ants rallied and made a final assault; now it was clear they would be the victors, and in the end so it was: the ants defeated the lizards in that great battle.

That is how friendship perished between ants and lizards, and it explains how it is that today you will never see the two creatures associating with one another. But ants will always swarm over the body of a dead lizard to pick it clean.

GALO AND VASIRI

This legend is well known in many of the coastal villages near Port Moresby, where the houses stand over the salt water on tilted posts, and the seagulls fly over the waves, diving for fish.

Long, long ago, before the time of the oldest tribesman's great-grandfather, there were two brothers, Galo and Vasiri, who lived in the same village. Galo was several years older than Vasiri, who was only about nine years old, with short legs and a big belly. Their parents had died, and Galo looked after his young brother like a father. Then, Galo married a woman called Gaiva, and the three of them lived together in the same house. Galo's love for his young brother did not grow less; but Gaiva hated Vasiri. She was a barren woman: no children were born to her, and she became bitter. She longed to have a child of her own, instead of having to care for young Vasiri, her husband's brother.

When Galo was out hunting with the other men of the village, Gaiva made Vasiri do all the house chores, and go to the garden to weed and dig vegetables. She made him cook the food, too, and when it was ready she would

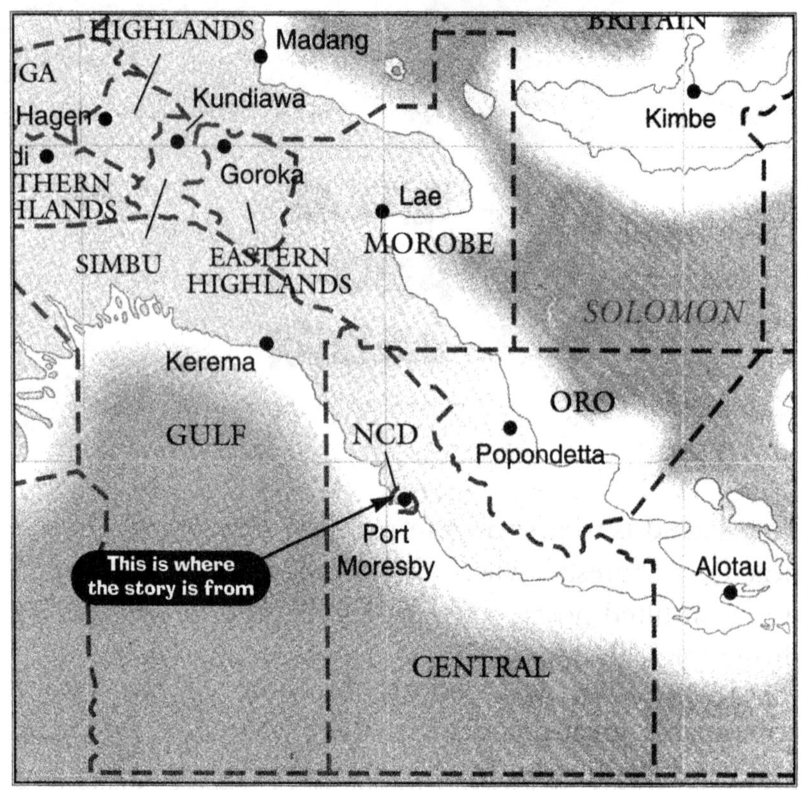

***Galo and Vasiri* was contributed by Mavara Ao Sere. Mavara comes from Hanuabada village near Port Moresby in the National Capital District.**

send him out of the house and then eat it all herself, so that when Vasiri returned, he would find only scraps. He would look in each cooking pot in turn, his belly rumbling with hunger. This always made Gaiva angry, and she would shout at him and tell him to look for food in the bush if he wanted something to eat. Then, sad and unhappy, Vasiri would search for mangoes and pawpaws in the bush, and he ate them even if they were green and unripe. If he couldn't find any food, he would go hungry all day, and cry himself to sleep at night.

When Galo was home, however, Gaiva would pretend to be kind to Vasiri; then she did the house chores and worked in the garden, and Vasiri got plenty to eat. He did not tell Galo about the way Gaiva treated him when he was away hunting, for he did not want to hurt his elder brother's pride, or break his love for his wife.

From week to week they continued in this way, until one fateful day. Galo was away from home, and, as usual, Gaiva chased Vasiri out of the house and told him to go and find some food for himself. Meanwhile, she ate the fish, yams and sago he had cooked for her.

Vasiri did not go straight to the bush; first, he tried to join in a game the other village boys were playing outside, but they told him to go away. 'We don't want to play with a boy who does women's work!' they jeered.

So, hungry and sad, Vasiri wandered into the bush, feeling twice as wretched as before. He sat under a talia tree, and ate some of the sweet nuts that clustered on its branches. Then, as though by magic, he suddenly saw an old woman standing before him: he recognised her as the wise woman who had been a friend to his dead parents, and whom they had trusted to make sure no harm came to their sons. He gazed at her, his face still wet with tears. Pity and tenderness showed in her eyes as she asked him why he was sad. Then, Vasiri told her the whole of his unhappiness: how Gaiva ill-treated him when Galo was away from home; how he was always hungry, and how the village boys despised him.

The old woman felt a great sadness in her heart for the boy; she told him that she would always be ready to help him, and that if he wanted her help, he was to return to the talia tree, where she would come to him.

Vasiri dried his eyes and felt comforted. He went home, and at sunset Galo returned from the hunting grounds, so that there was plenty to eat that evening. But in spite of his full belly, Vasiri found it difficult to get to sleep that night. He lay with his eyes open, gazing up at the thatched roof. His thoughts were long and deep, and at last they resolved themselves into a strange plan in his mind. Just before dawn, the boy got up and crept quietly outside the house. In the cool, dark morning he walked through the bush until he came to the talia tree, and when he got there he sat on the ground, leaning against its trunk. And still two opposing thoughts filled his mind: his brother's love for himself and for Gaiva, and Gaiva's cruelty to him.

A light wind rustled through the talia leaves; there stood the wise old woman.

'I need your help,' Vasiri told her. He looked down at the ground. 'I have thought and thought,' he said, 'and I have decided that I would like you to turn me into a fish. Then, I can live under the sea, where Gaiva will never to able to find me and torment me.'

The old woman did not reply at once. Then, in a

troubled voice, she said that she would grant his wish. She told him that he was to walk backwards to the sea, his face turned towards the village, singing one line of a song for each step he took. And she told him the words of the song he was to sing. Vasiri, overjoyed, thanked her for her help, and she disappeared again as magically as she had come to him. Vasiri, who was very tired after his restless night, fell asleep. When he awoke the day was nearly over; soon it would be dusk. It was time for him to go to the sea. First, however, he went back to the house to say goodbye to his brother; but Galo had gone hunting that day and only Gaiva was at home.

'Your brother will return at sunset,' she told Vasiri. 'Don't let me see you until he gets back.'

'You will never see me again,' Vasiri thought in his heart; and now he began his walk to the sea, going backwards, his face turned to the village which he was leaving for ever. At each step, he sang a line of the song the old woman had taught him.

Away in the forest, Galo was coming home, striding through the bush carrying his spear, a pig flung over his shoulder. Suddenly, he felt a strange sensation in his arm, as though he were being stung by a hundred ants: this was the very moment that Vasiri had begun to sing his song. Straight away, Galo knew that something bad was happening to his young brother, his beloved Vasiri. He began to run as swiftly as he could. As he neared the village, he heard the faint sound of his brother's voice, and soon he was able to make out the words he was singing:

'All the time, my dear brother Galo,
While you were away hunting for meat,
O beloved brother, your wife Gaiva

Fed me with scraps of food
Or sent me into the bush
To see what I could find.'

By this time, Vasiri had taken his first step backwards into the shallow water that lapped the shore. As he went on, the sea got deeper: it covered his ankles . . . his knees . . . his thighs . . .

Galo reached the place where his brother had begun his walk to the sea. And still Vasiri sang:

'Gaiva was always cruel to me:
She made me work in the house;
She made me work in the garden.
The village boys despised me.
When you were home, Galo,
She pretended to love me.'

Now Vasiri was right out on the reef; the water had reached his armpits.

'I shall become a fish under the blue sea:
Deep in the sea I shall swim and be happy.
Come and look for me, beloved brother!'

In grief and despair Galo called to Vasiri and told him to come back, come back, come back! But Vasiri did not hear him. As he sang the last words of his song, the water closed over his head and he disappeared beneath the sea.

For a long time Galo stood staring at the place where his brother had vanished; then he returned to his house. His head was filled with mingled sorrow for his brother and hatred for his wife. And, in his memory, Vasiri's last words sounded clearly: 'Come and look for me, beloved brother!'

Gaiva was in the house making the fire when Galo entered, his spear held ready in his hand. With no warning, no pity and no more love for his wife, he flung the spear at Gaiva: it struck her through the heart and she died instantly.

Then Galo went into the bush, to the very place beneath the talia tree where Vasiri had met the wise woman. There he sat in despair; and presently she appeared before him, just as she had come to his brother, with the same pity and tenderness showing in her gaze.

'Turn me into a bird!' Galo begged her. 'Then I can fly over the sea to find my brother, Vasiri the fish.'

The old woman performed this magic in an instant: in place of Galo the brave hunter there was a small, white-feathered bird with strong wings and a curved beak. Uttering a shrill cry, Galo the seagull flew straight across the water to the spot where he had seen his brother disappear. He flew around until he saw a fish in the sea below, and dived down to it. But it was not Vasiri his brother. Angry, he caught the fish in his beak and ate it in one gulp, then flew on over the sea, still searching for Vasiri.

Today, when Galo the seagull flies over the sea, diving down every now and then to pluck a fish from the water, he is still looking for his brother Vasiri the fish. He has not found him yet—and every time he discovers that the fish he has spied is not his brother, he swallows it whole.

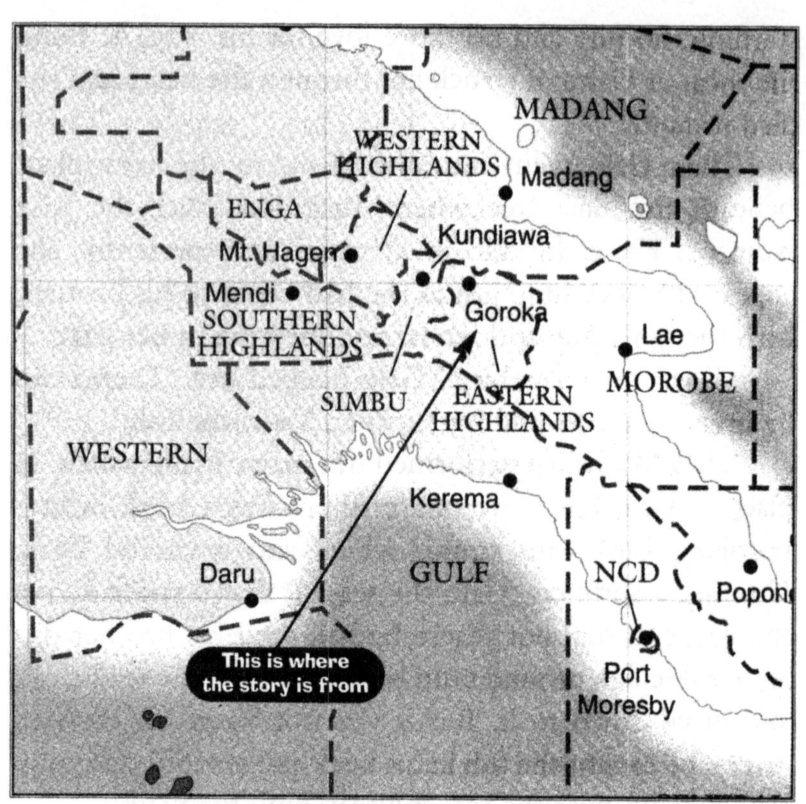

The Greedy Dogs was contributed by Eric E. Oso. Eric comes from Moke village in the Eastern Highlands Province.

THE GREEDY DOGS

In the Eastern Highlands, not far from Fore, there is a curious round rock. The people who live in this area tell a story about the rock, a story which belongs to the time long ago when creatures lived in houses, talked to each other, and were able to use fire and cook their food. At that time, the wallabies and the dogs, strange as it may seem, were good friends; they lived together in a big round house which they had built. The walls were of tree bark, and the roof was thatched with palm. The wallabies, like the dogs, used to run about on all four legs in those days.

Both the wallabies and the dogs went hunting each day. The dogs were the better hunters, but they did not share their food with the wallabies. In fact, they used to eat it as soon as they caught the creature they were hunting—a wild pig, perhaps, a possum, or maybe a cassowary. The wallabies, on the other hand, brought home their meat to cook before they ate it, and always shared it with dogs, even though they did not catch so much.

In this way they lived together for several years; but at last the wallabies became so disgusted with the dogs' behaviour that they decided not to share their food with them any longer.

One day the wallabies came home from hunting earlier than the dogs, and they held a meeting to discuss the situation. At last all their unhappy feelings about the dogs were revealed, as one wallaby after another spoke out.

'The dogs are greedy and selfish!'

'The dogs eat their meat raw and have smelly mouths!'

'The dogs take our food, even though their bellies are already full when they come home!'

So they went on, saying bad things about the dogs in loud, angry tones. They did not realise that a sick dog lay quietly in a dark part of the house, listening to everything they said. He had been left behind when the other dogs went hunting that day. He lay there, his head resting on his paws, and said nothing. But he remembered all the words that were spoken by the wallabies.

The wallabies, having decided not to share their food with the dogs any longer, then cooked and ate everything they had caught that day. Not a scrap was left.

Presently all the other dogs came home; they ran into the house, smelling of the meat they had already eaten, looking forward to helping themselves to the wallabies' food as well. When they found out that the wallabies had eaten it all, they growled and barked to show their anger. 'What is the meaning of this?' asked the chief dog.

Then the sick dog spoke up. 'I can tell you!' he said. 'While you were out hunting, the wallabies held a meeting and said terrible things about us: how greedy and selfish we are, and how we smell—and they decided they would never share their food with us again.'

'Did they indeed!' snarled the chief dog.

The wallabies began to feel very frightened; they were not as strong as the dogs and knew they might be killed if the dogs attacked them. But how could they escape from the house? The largest and fiercest of the dogs stood in the doorway, and there were no windows, only small, natural holes in the tree-bark walls.

Suddenly the dogs sprang upon the wallabies, biting and snapping at them; the wallabies, in a panic, flung themselves at the walls, scrabbling at the bark and breaking them down, then squeezing through any opening in order to escape; and they all broke their forelegs as they did so. Most of them were killed by the dogs; only a few escaped, and they hopped away on their hind legs into the bush, where they have lived ever since. They were never able to go about on four legs again, and now all wallabies hold their short front legs before them as they leap from place to place.

After the fight, the dogs burned down the round house, and when the smoke cleared, a big round rock stood in its place, which remains there to this day. Then, the dogs made a vow that they would chase and kill all wallabies whenever they came upon them: and that is how dogs and wallabies became enemies.

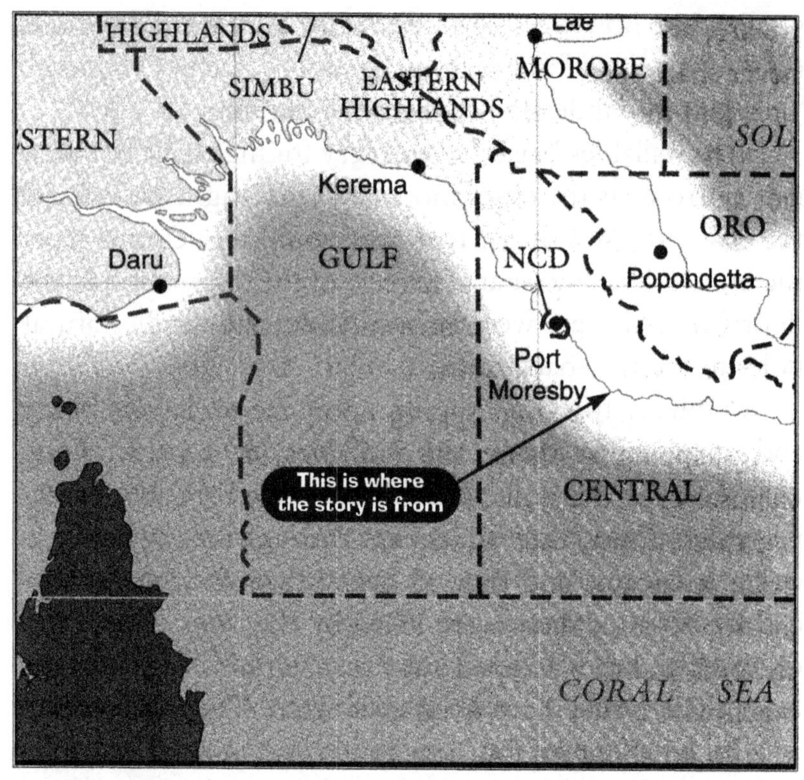

The Cockatoo's Head-Dress **was contributed by Aloysius Aihi. Aloysius comes from Tsiria village in the Central Province.**

THE COCKATOO'S HEAD-DRESS

Many, many years ago, a little village called Ario sat on the bank of the River Boho Biro—the River of Giving. The people called the river Boho Biro because it gave them water to irrigate their land, and so they were able to plant gardens and grow good crops. Everyone in the village was contented and considered himself fortunate except for one inhabitant—Beau'ari the Cockatoo, who had been caught in the forest, and had been a prisoner for a long time. He was kept in a bamboo cage outside the chief's house. He had tried to escape, but it was no use: the bars of his cage were too strong. He did not look as cockatoos do today; his head was as flat as a seagull's.

One day, the people of Ario village began to prepare for a feast. The music-makers practised their flute playing and beat upon the kundu drums; the dancers practised their steps, and all the villagers made ready their body decorations and ornaments: necklaces of shells and dogs' teeth, bracelets of woven grass and kangaroo fur, nose-bones, and head-dresses of red and yellow feathers, and straw stuck with shiny green beetles. The chief had the most gorgeous head-dress of all: a magnificent crest of bright yellow feathers which made him stand taller than all the other tribesmen.

On the day itself, the women went to the gardens to gather fruit and vegetables and the men went off fishing, or to hunt in the forest for meat. The only living beings left in the village, besides the tame pigs and a few lazy dogs (and Beau'ari the Cockatoo) were three small children. One was the youngest of the chief's many sons.

The children spent the morning playing, and then the chief's son took the two other boys home to find some food. But they could find nothing to eat, nothing at all, and because they were so young, and very hungry, they sat on the platform outside the house and cried. There they sat, three boys in a row, with tears rolling down their faces. Then, above the noise they were making, one of the boys heard the sound of soft singing.

'Stop crying!' he told the other two. 'Listen!'

The three of them listened, their ears pricked like a hunting dog's. And they all heard the words of a well-loved dancing song:

'Poe—Raria Maiva—Rapia Maiva
Taravatsu, Kemai Rarevo Manevo
Tsiumaio Poe.'

Poe—Raria Maiva, Rapia Maiva
Let be! Let him come and alight!
Come, Poe!

(*Poe is the name of a bird; Raria Maiva, Rapia Maiva are proper names, in this case given to the bird.*)

They looked up and down and all around to see who could be singing this song so beautifully, and suddenly they realised that the singer was Beau'ari the Cockatoo, in his bamboo cage. They went up to his cage and asked him to sing some more. The cockatoo was a clever fellow, and now he made up a cunning plan to escape from his captivity.

'I would like to sing some more for you,' he told the boys, 'but I always sing much more sweetly if I am wearing a head-dress, as though I were at a feast.'

The chief's son thought at once of his father's splendid head-dress of yellow feathers, which hung on one wall of the house. He ran inside to fetch it, and held it up for the cockatoo to see.

'Will this do?' he asked.

'It will do very well,' said the cockatoo. 'But I'm afraid I won't be able to wear it inside this cage—there isn't enough room.'

'That's easy,' said the boys, 'we'll let you out of the cage, then you'll have plenty of room.'

So they let the cockatoo out of the bamboo cage, and carefully fitted the head-dress on his smooth flat white head. How handsome Beau'ari looked now! He strutted up and down the platform, and, true to his promise, he sang again for the boys:

'Kororo—Kororo—Banimu papare
Emu rari papakia no hara'au hara'au
Nini mobiomobio—Nini mobiomobio—Nana mobiomobio, Kororo.'

'Kororo, Kororo! Your wings are plucked.
You peck at the grains of sand.
Necklaced bird, Necklaced bird,
Kororo.'

(*Kororo and Nini are the names of birds.*)

The three boys, who had by now quite forgotten their hunger and their disappointment at finding no food to eat, laughed and applauded the cockatoo's singing, jumping up and down in their excitement.

Presently, the men who had been fishing returned from the sea, carrying long strings of gleaming fish for the feast. They saw the three boys jumping up and down outside the chief's house, and ran over to them, wondering what had happened. As soon as the cockatoo saw the fishermen, he fled to the top of a coconut palm, with the yellow head-dress still perched on his head.

'Men of Ario!' he called down to them, 'you have kept me a prisoner for a long time. Now I am free! And I will pay you back for my long captivity by destroying all your crops.' Then, he tried to take off the yellow head-dress, meaning to throw it to the ground, but the boys had placed it so firmly on his head that he couldn't move it.

To this very day, you will still see the cockatoo wearing the chief's head-dress, which is the bright yellow crest upon his head. Often you will see a whole flock of cockatoos swoop down upon a garden, squawking and chattering in shrill voices very different to Beau'ari's sweet singing. They are fulfilling the threat made to the villagers of Ario so long ago—they have come to destroy the crops.

THE TURTLE WIFE

In New Ireland, banana trees grow in abundance. Every day, children run down to the edge of the sea with many-fingered bunches of the fruit, to wash them before they are cooked. The tree takes several months to bear fruit: it must first grow and bear its crown of long, fringed leaves. Then, a long spike of yellow flowers appears, and these flowers turn into the fruit which is so good to eat: not the large, sweet-tasting banana, but small bananas that are baked in their skins while they are green. After the banana tree has borne its fruit it withers and dies, but other trees spring up from the suckers beneath the ground.

This story belongs to a time when the people of New Ireland were just beginning to cultivate food gardens, instead of gathering all their vegetables and fruit from the wild bush. Then, as today, the sea provided most of their food, for they were always great fishermen, harvesting strings of shining fish in their canoes fashioned from the pliant wood of the erema tree.

It happened one day in that long-ago time that a certain young man decided to go fishing in the deeper part of the sea, far from the shore. He wanted to catch a big fish

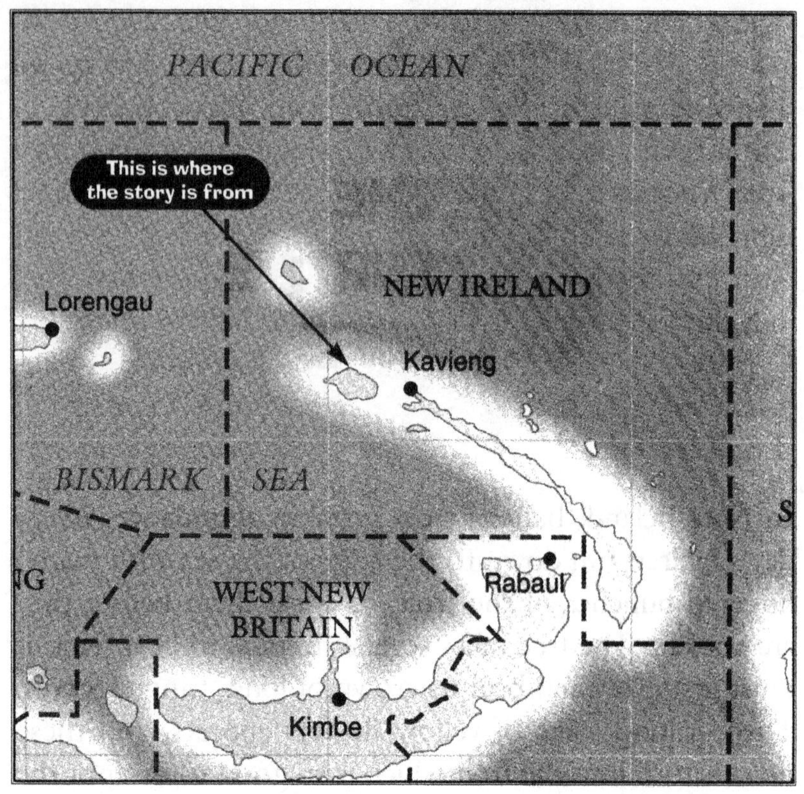

The Turtle Wife **was contributed by Paraide Revi. Paraide comes from Taskul village, on an island near New Hanover, in the New Ireland Province. She attended Madina High School, before going on to the University of Technology, Lae, to study accountancy and business studies.**

that would provide him with plenty of food, for he was hungry. He lived alone, with no wife to help him plant a food garden, and often it was difficult to find food in the wild bush. He placed his fishing line, spear, and some bait wrapped in a large leaf in his canoe, and paddled out to that deep water where the big fishes lived. There he threw his line into the sea; he let it out and out, farther and farther, until all that was left was the end which he grasped in his hands.

For a long while nothing happened. The sun rose overhead and the young fisherman grew hot and drowsy. Hunger pains cramped his stomach, for he had eaten nothing before he lay down to sleep the night before, nothing when he arose that morning. His eyelids drooped, his hands slackened their grip on the fishing line . . . when suddenly he was jerked wide-awake by a tremendous tug on the line that almost pulled him right out of the canoe. Quickly he began to haul in the line, pulling with all his strength. At last his catch broke through the surface of the sea. It was a large female turtle!

Disappointed that he had not caught the big fish he had hoped for, the young man debated whether he should take the turtle home or put it back in the sea. Imagine his amazement when the turtle spoke to him, saying: 'Please put me back into the sea. If you do, I will help you in whatever way you like.'

But the young man thought he would like to keep the turtle after all; he decided to take her home to see what would happen and whether she would continue to talk to him. 'After all,' he thought, 'I am a lonely man, living by myself. It is better to have a turtle to talk to than no one at all.'

So he paddled back to the shore in his canoe, beached it, then lifted the turtle on to his shoulders and went back to his house. And now he thought: 'Perhaps this turtle will marry me, for it is better to marry a turtle than have no wife at all.'

The next day he asked the turtle if she would marry him. Shyly the turtle agreed to have him as her husband; but she told him he must wait a while before she took off her turtle shell and came to him as a woman.

'But tell me,' she said, 'why is it that you have so little to eat? You are thin and hungry, and there is no food in your house.'

'I am poor,' the young man told her. 'My brothers do not think of me, but keep all their food for themselves. I depend on my fishing and gather food from the wild bush to keep myself alive. I would make a food garden, but there is no one to help me look after it, to plant it and weed it while I go fishing.'

'I am with you now,' the turtle said in her soft voice. 'I will help you tend a food garden.'

So they decided to make a garden. In the cool of the morning, the young man set off into the bush, with the turtle on his shoulders as before, and carrying the tools he needed for clearing the ground. He kept walking, looking everywhere for a good place to make his garden, and at last he found the right spot, close by a small hill. He left the turtle on the side of the hill and began to clear the ground. By the end of the day he had finished his work, and then the man and the turtle returned to their house.

They came again to the garden the next day, and this time the man brought the tools he needed for digging and hoeing, as well as taro suckers and potato cuttings for planting. Again he left the turtle on the hill, and, while her husband's back was turned to her as he dug and hoed and planted, she emerged from her shell as a beautiful woman and came to help him in his work. And now, how glad the young man was that he had chosen his turtle wife from the sea!

'*I have brought you a special plant, husband,*' *she told* him, showing him a sucker different to that of the taro, and different to any other plant he had ever seen before. 'I will plant it here in our garden, and you shall see it grow, first into one tree, then into many trees that will bear delicious and nourishing fruit, not only for ourselves, but for all the people who live in this place. The name of the tree and of the fruit is banana.'

And so the turtle wife of the young fisherman planted the first banana tree in that place. At the end of that day she returned to her shell once more, and her husband carried her back to their home as he had done before.

So it continued: each morning they went to work in their garden and each evening they returned home again. Their garden grew and prospered, and they were happy and content with each other's company. And the banana sucker which the turtle wife had planted began to grow, sending up a slender trunk which became a little higher each day.

But the young fisherman's brothers had been watching him. They were curious to know why he went off to the bush each day, and returned each night, carrying a turtle on his shoulders. One morning, they followed him all the way to the garden he had made. They saw the turtle slip out of her shell and emerge as a beautiful woman to help her husband hoe and weed the plants they had grown. They saw that she was more beautiful by far than their own wives, and they felt jealous of their brother and his turtle wife, and the fine garden they had made together. On the other side of the hill they lit a big fire, and then they stole the turtle shell and thrust it into the fire, and it began to burn.

At the end of the day, the turtle wife came to the place where she had left her shell and discovered it had gone. She smelt smoke and went to the other side of the hill, where her husband's brothers were raking up the ashes of the fire they had lit. She was just in time to see the last bit of her shell smouldering away. Sad and angry, she told the brothers that they had acted wrongly and foolishly.

'In our garden,' she told them, 'I have sown a banana plant, from which in time many trees will grow, all bearing fruit to feed you and your children and your children's children. This banana tree would have borne its fruit in a very little while, as soon as it sent out its first two leaves. But now, to punish you for burning my shell, you must wait a long time for that first fruit. Now the tree must grow a crown of many leaves and a spike of yellow flowers before the fruit comes at last.'

Ever since that day, the banana tree has grown just as the turtle wife decreed; and, as she promised, innumerable trees have sprung from that first plant, their fruit feeding generations beyond count descended from those long-ago people who lived in the place we now call New Ireland.

CASSOWARY AND KOKOMO

The cassowary and the kokomo, or hornbill, are two of the most familiar birds of Papua New Guinea. Today, the cassowary is a bird with small, useless wings that always lives on the ground. It is able to run very fast and to swim, but it cannot fly. The kokomo, the hornbill, is smaller than the big cassowary, and has a croaking voice; it flaps its wings noisily as it flies from tree to tree. Both the cassowary and the kokomo wear large crests upon their heads.

But it was not always so. Once upon a time, long ago, it was the cassowary which flew through the forest, while the kokomo lived on the ground. In that far-off time they were good friends, and the kokomo always built his nest at the foot of the tree where the cassowary chose to live.

One day, the cassowary discovered a new area of the forest where food was plentiful and there were few other creatures to compete for it. 'We should make our home in that place!' he told the kokomo.

'But we have a good home here,' the kokomo protested.

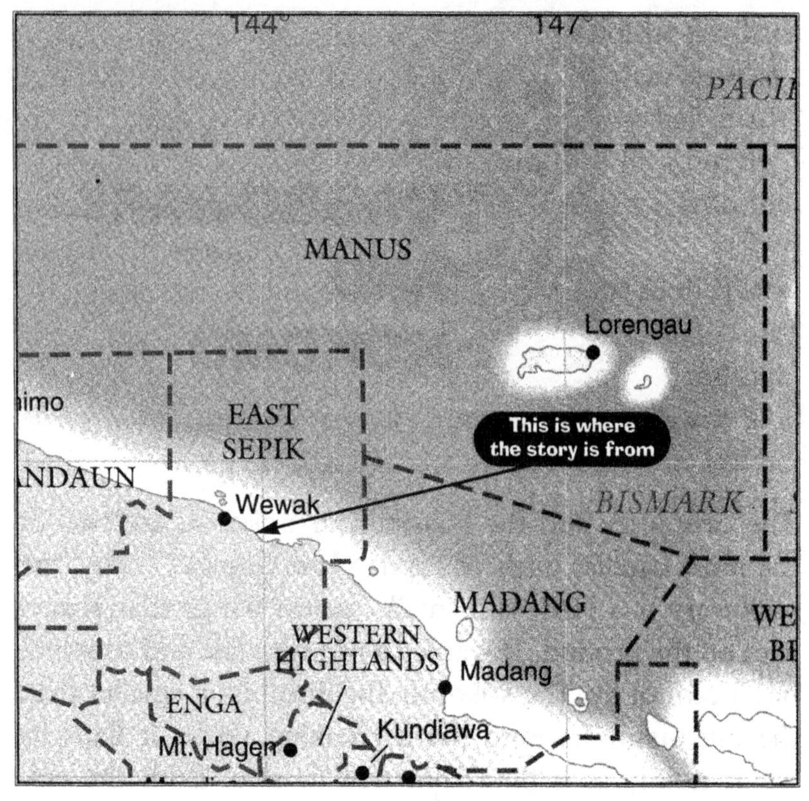

Cassowary And Kokomo **was contributed by Joseph Wapidu. Joseph comes from Makepin village in the East Sepik Province. He attended St. Xavier's High School, before going on to the University of Technology, Lae.**

'We would have a better home there,' said the cassowary.

'It's all very well for you,' grumbled the kokomo, 'you are able to fly above the trees free as air: it is nothing for you to get from one place to another. But I must go over the ground, and the way to this new place is long and difficult.'

In the end, however, the cassowary persuaded the kokomo to leave their old home for the new one, and early the next morning they both set off. It took the cassowary only a short while to reach the new place in the forest, for he could fly straight to it above the tree-tops; but the kokomo, who could not fly, had to travel uphill and downhill, through valleys and across rivers, and by the time he arrived it was almost dark and he was exhausted. All the while, as he journeyed, his thoughts had become more and more bitter, and he had grown more and more jealous of the cassowary, who was able to fly while he could not.

'There you are at last!' the cassowary greeted him from the highest branch of a tall tree. 'What a long time you have been! I have been dozing in this tree all day, waiting for you to turn up!'

The kokomo was filled with rage when he heard these words, and thought of how the cassowary had been resting most of the day, while he toiled over his hard journey. All his bitter and jealous thoughts spilled over, and he decided to discover a way in which he could destroy the cassowary's ability to fly.

Both birds settled down for the night in the new home, the cassowary at the top of that tall tree, and the kokomo at its foot.

Next day, the kokomo visited the wise tree-beetle. 'Please help me,' the kokomo said. 'I can no longer bear the cassowary's arrogance and thoughtlessness.'

That night, while the cassowary was sleeping, perched on a high branch, the tree-beetle climbed up and with its needle-sharp snout bored so many holes in the branch that at last it gave way, and the cassowary fell to the ground with a loud thump. He was so badly injured that he knew he would never be able to fly again.

The kokomo felt sorry for the cassowary and the tree-beetle gave him medicine to heal his friend's hurts; the beetle also transferred to the kokomo the flying magic that had belonged to the cassowary, so that now the kokomo was able to flap his wings and rise into the air, and flit from tree to tree as the cassowary used to do.

Today, kokomos still fly, while cassowaries keep to the ground—and if you go to the hollow trees in which kokomos build their nests, you will see cassowaries feeding on the ground beneath them.

THE ISLAND AND THE RIVER

The old people who live alongside the Sepik River and the elders whose home is Manam Island, which sits in the sea off the northern coast of Papua New Guinea, tell this story to their children to explain where Manam Island came from, and how the Sepik River was formed.

There were once, so long ago that a man's tongue would drop from his mouth if he tried to number the seasons that have passed since that time, two big mountains. They stood close beside each other, inland from the coast. They were brothers, these two mountains, for in those days a mountain might also be a man, and their names were Auroka and Manam. Auroka, the elder, was taller and stronger than Manam. Their parents had died and after they had gone, neither Auroka, the elder brother, nor Manam, the younger, knew which of them should rightfully own the different pieces of land and the various goods their parents had left behind.

One day, Manam decided to make a new garden; he chose a certain place in the forest, and began to cut down the trees with his stone axe, clearing a level patch of ground surrounded by cedar and kwila trees and tall

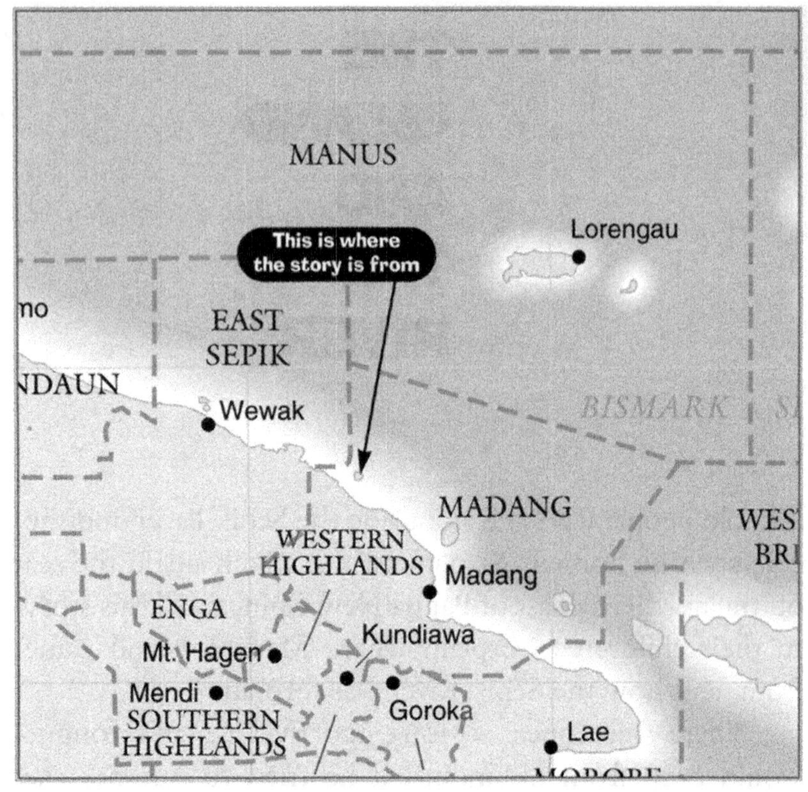

The Island And The River **was contributed by Jave Bom. Jave comes from Budua village on Manam Island in the Madang Province. He attended Tusbab High School, before going on to the University of Technology, Lae, to study accountancy and business studies.**

eucalypts. As he worked, hacking and chopping at the tough vines, he thought of the plants he would bring to the garden: plantains and bananas, taro and breadfruit, yams and sago palms.

Suddenly Auroka walked into the clearing, his face filled with anger. 'What are you doing?' he shouted. 'This is my land!'

Manam looked up, astonished at his brother's anger. 'I am going to make a new garden here,' he said quietly.

'Not here! This is my land!' Auroka shouted. 'Go to your own land and make a garden.'

Manam was puzzled. 'But which is my land, and which is yours, brother?' he asked. 'I did not think this piece of earth was yours. In any case, I will share my garden with you, if you wish. Must I move to another piece of land? Surely there is plenty for us to share in peace.'

Manam's calm manner seemed to make Auroka even more furious. When he heard those words, he choked with rage. 'Get out of my sight!' he shouted. 'Go! Out of my sight, before I kill you!'

Manam was very sad when he heard his brother speak these words. He began to weep. 'Brothers should not kill each other,' he said. 'Why do you want to harm me? Why should we not live happily together?'

'I don't care whether you are my brother or not,' Auroka shouted. His eyes blazed with fury. 'Just get out of here—go right away, where I can't see you!'

A heavy grief fell upon Manam. He did not want to leave the land where he had been born, but obeyed his elder brother and began to move slowly towards the sea. And as he went, his passage formed a V-shaped trench in the ground. At last he reached the edge of the sea, where he turned round and looked backwards and upward to where Auroka stood watching him.

'I can still see you!' Auroka called. 'Go farther still! Out of my sight!'

So Manam plunged into the sea, and swam through the water for one hundred kilometres or more. And still Auroka's voice sounded faintly from the land: 'Farther, farther still! Out of my sight!'

At last Manam reached a place in the sea where he could no longer hear his brother's voice—the place where Manam Island now stands. His feet touched the seabed and he stands there still, facing towards the land that used to be his home.

At sunset on that long-ago day when Auroka chased his brother out of his sight, when the clouds clustered red and gold and brown about the mountain peaks, just before darkness came, Auroka looked down from his great height and saw the path Manam had made, the clear-cut V-shaped trench that led down to the sea. Suddenly he felt ashamed, and a great sadness entered into him. He began to weep. He wept so mightily and for such a long time that his tears dripped down his vast mountainside, and flowed in a great channel along the trench made by his brother.

Today, the Sepik River still flows along the track which was made by Manam and filled with the tears of his brother Auroka. And beside the mountain that was Auroka is the place where Manam once stood, who now sits as an island in the middle of the sea.

BILAK POKIS

Bilak Pokis—Black Fox—was the name of a fisherman who once, a long time ago, lived alone on Rarah Island, offshore from Lorengau. Sometimes, when Bilak Pokis was tired of fishing, he would get into his canoe and paddle across to the mainland to hunt for meat.

One season, the small island that was Bilak Pokis' home was battered by a series of bad storms. Unable to find any fish in the troubled waters, he ran out of food. There was nothing to do but to set out for the mainland. He pushed his canoe into the sea, put all his tools and weapons on board, and began to paddle across the water. But before he had gone very far the big waves swamped his canoe, and in a few moments it sank beneath the sea. Bilak Pokis managed to grab his knife, and swam back to the island holding it in his teeth. He waded to the shore, then sat on a log and wondered what to do next. If he did not get to the mainland he would surely starve. He looked up, and beyond the reef he saw a bird flying off a floating log, heading for the mainland.

'If only I could fly like that bird, I would soon reach the mainland,' he said to himself; and no sooner had this

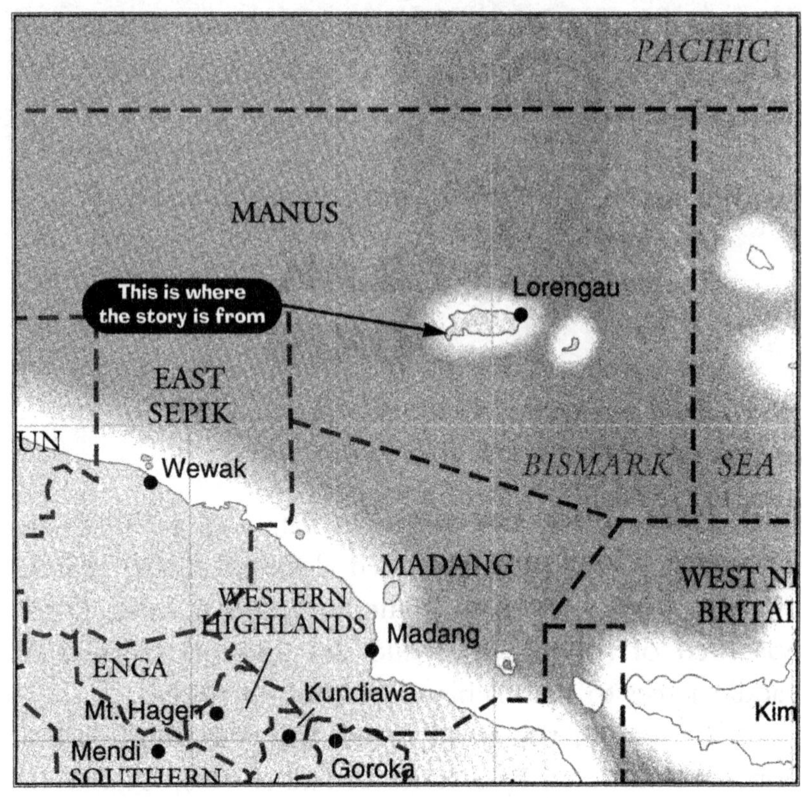

Bilak Pokis **was contributed by David Pondris. David comes from M'Bunai in the Manus Province.**

thought come to him than he jumped to his feet and began to look for some material he could use to make a pair of wings.

A tall coconut palm grew on the island. Nothing was impossible in those long-ago days, and Bilak Pokis was not very surprised, therefore, when this tree suddenly spoke to him.

'What are you looking for?' it asked, bending toward him.

'I want to make a pair of wings for myself, so that I may fly to the mainland and hunt food,' Bilak Pokis replied.

'I can help you,' the tree said. 'Climb my trunk and cut some of my branches, then weave my palm fronds together like a mat. If you tie these to your arms, you will have a very good pair of wings.'

Bilak Pokis wasted no time. He climbed up the slender trunk of the coconut palm and cut some branches with his knife. Then, he set to weaving the fronds together, and soon he had made himself a huge pair of wings, which he tied to his arms. Then, from the very top of that tall tree, he launched himself into the air, and found himself flying like a bird towards the mainland. Halfway there, however, the wind began to blow through the palm matting he had woven, and he found it was very hard going. In spite of this he reached the mainland safely, and landed on a river bank. Here, he scooped up some damp clay and daubed it all over his wings. He waited until the clay dried in the hot sun then set off once more, flying towards a place where he knew he would find good hunting. But it was farther than he remembered; he felt tired, and decided to rest in a tree. This, however, was difficult; the weight of the clay daubed on his wings unbalanced him. Each time he tried to sit upright on a branch, he ended by hanging head-downward.

'The coconut tree has made a fool of me!' he thought angrily. 'These stupid wings make me look ridiculous, hanging head-down!' And Bilak Pokis began to plan how he could get his revenge.

Now when Bilak Pokis put on his wings on that far-off day, he turned himself into a flying fox; and today all flying foxes hang upside-down on the branches of trees. Furthermore, whenever a flying fox lands on a coconut palm, it will attack the young nuts—this is the way it takes its revenge upon the tree that first supplied it with wings. You will very seldom see a flying fox during the day, because they are ashamed to show their ugly wings, which Bilak Pokis daubed with wet clay so long ago. They fly about after the sun has set, when darkness falls across the sky and over the land. The flying fox is now called blakbokis.

THE TUMARANG'S REVENGE

The small island of Matupit lies off the east coast of New Britain, near Rabaul. The people of Matupit tell this story about the volcano which sits on their island, at a place called Raulavat.

A long, long time ago, there was no volcano on Matupit Island. The ground was flat, and it happened that in the very place where the volcano is now, a man called Tavuvur and his wife, Ngeok, decided to plant a new garden to grow their food. The foods from their old garden were becoming poor both in quantity and quality; the same earth had been used for growing for too long. It was time to start afresh. So they got into their canoe and paddled off to Raulavat, where they began to clear the ground, cutting down the undergrowth and the trees so that they might plant their new crops. As Ngeok toiled, she thought of the time when the new crops would yield their harvests of taro, yams, bananas, breadfruit, and kaukau, the sweet potato. Ngeok and Tavuvur worked hard all day and were pleased with their efforts, but there was one big, old fig-tree that Tavuvur could not cut down,

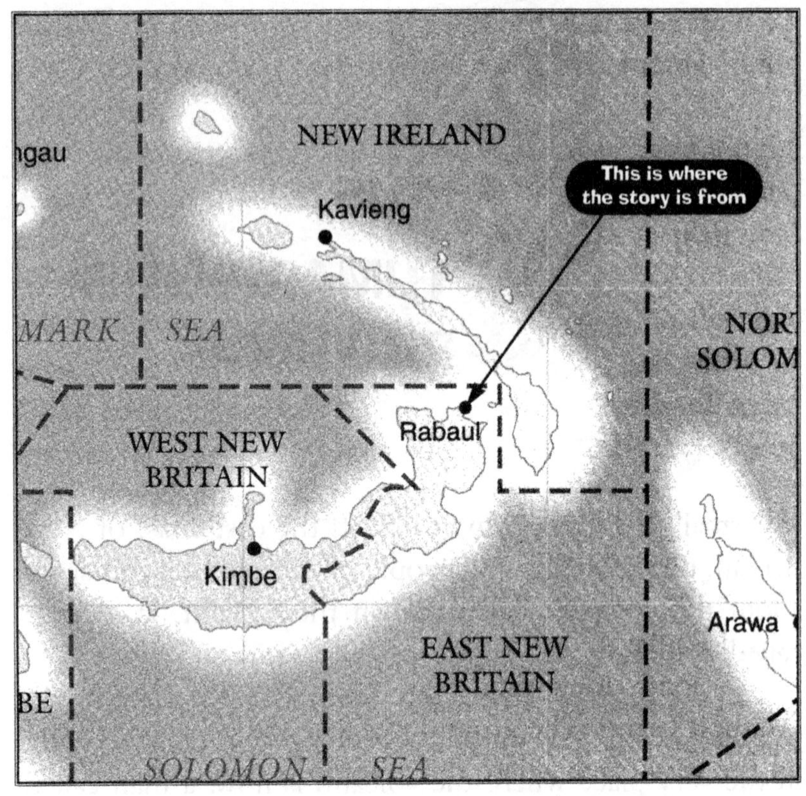

The Tumarang's Revenge **was contributed by Skerry Palanga. Skerry comes from Rabaul in the East New Britain Province. He attended Rabaul High School, before going on to the University of Technology, Lae, to study surveying.**

even though he used all his strength to chop at the trunk with his keen-edged axe of stone.

'The only way to get rid of this tree is to burn it down,' he told Ngeok at last, gasping for breath.

So they lit a fire at the foot of the tree, then stood back to watch as the fierce flames swallowed the trunk, the limbs, and the leaves of the fig-tree.

They did not know that the fig-tree was the home of the dreaded Tumarang, an evil spirit who was away hunting when Tavuvur and Ngeok came to that place to make their garden. At sunset, the Tumarang returned. His anger, when he saw that his home had been destroyed, was terrible to see.

Using strong magic, the Tumarang made a high stone hill rise out of the ground, over the place where the fig-tree had stood, and he trapped Tavuvur and Ngeok inside the hill, which was hollow. Tavuvur himself knew some magic, but it was not as strong as the Tumarang's magic. Nevertheless, he attacked the Tumarang; inside the hill, the two of them fought and raged against each other while Ngeok looked on fearfully. Suddenly there was a vast explosion: stones, great slabs of earth and fire from the burnt-out fig tree were forced out of the top of the hill and showered down below, spreading out for a great distance, so that the people of Matupit and other nearby villages had to run as fast as a cassowary to escape to safety. Stones rained down from the hill and sparks of fire fell on to their houses, burning through the thatched roofs.

The Tumarang flew out of the hill when it exploded, but Tavuvur and Ngeok were still trapped inside it. They, too, tried to escape through the hole in the top; but the Tumarang had made sure that the sides of the hill were so steep that they could not climb out.

'What shall we do?' they asked each other in despair.

Then Ngeok had an idea. 'If only we could attract the notice of the villagers of Matupit, they would come and dig a tunnel through the side of this hill so that we might escape,' she said.

'How can we possibly attract the villagers' notice when we are imprisoned here?' Tavuvur asked.

'We can make a fire,' Ngeok said. 'It is the rainy season, and if we light a fire early in the morning, it will smoulder slowly and the smoke will go out through the hole in the top, as a signal to the people of Matupit.'

Tavuvur could not think of a better idea, and so they did as Ngeok suggested. It was many days before a group of ten boys was sent from Matupit to find out the meaning of the smoke signal that arose each morning from Raulavat. By this time, Tavuvur and Ngeok had grown very weak. The boys came to Raulavat by canoe. They beached their canoes, leaving the youngest boy, Tovue, to look after them, then came to the high hill that the Tumarang had made with his strong magic. The boys climbed to the very top of the hill and peered down the hole, through the smoke.

Tavuvur stood with difficulty and cupped his hands around his mouth so that his enfeebled voice might carry farther. 'Help us to get out of here!' he called. 'Dig a tunnel in the side of the hill so that we may crawl out!'

The boys were very surprised to hear Tavuvur's voice, but they agreed to dig the tunnel and began the work at once, using strong digging-sticks. But the Tumarang, the evil spirit, saw what was happening. Determined that no one should help Tavuvur and Ngeok to escape, he made the part of the hill where the boys were digging collapse on top of them, and they were all buried under a great heap of stones.

Only Tovue, guarding the canoes on the beach, was left to paddle back to Matupit and tell the villagers what had happened. There was great wailing and weeping in Matupit when Tovue told how the other boys had been buried in the side of the hill, and a party of strong men was sent to dig out their bodies and bring them home.

The men came to Raulavat and dug in the hillside. By now, both Tavuvur and Ngeok had perished inside their prison. Once again the Tumarang worked his magic: to the amazement of the villagers, when they had cleared away the fallen stones, instead of discovering the boys' bodies, nine birds the size of chickens, of a kind never seen before, flew out above their heads. The men dug down farther and found some strange eggs, each one twice the size of a chicken's egg.

Weary with digging, the villagers took some of the eggs and cooked them. They made very good eating, so they collected those that remained and took them back to Matupit to share with the rest of the village.

Ever since that day, the people of Matupit Island have gone across to Raulavat in their canoes to dig for those strange eggs in the hillside, where the birds still live. As for the hill itself, it stands there still, and is known today as Matupit volcano.

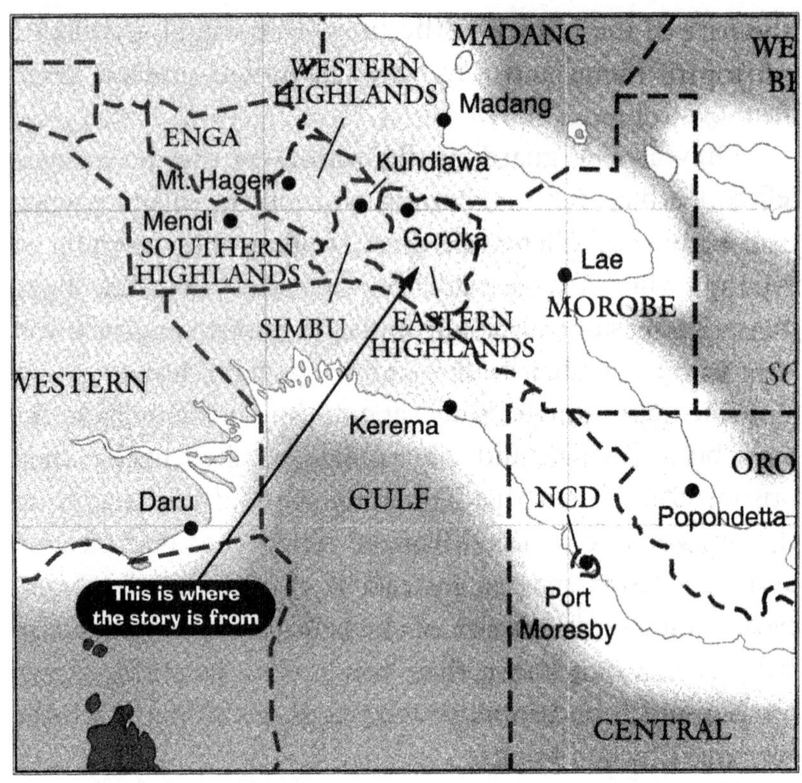

***Papaya* was contributed by Samira Unamba. Samira comes from Tapo village in the Eastern Highlands Province. He attended Asaroka High School, before going on to the University of Technology, Lae, to study electrical surveying.**

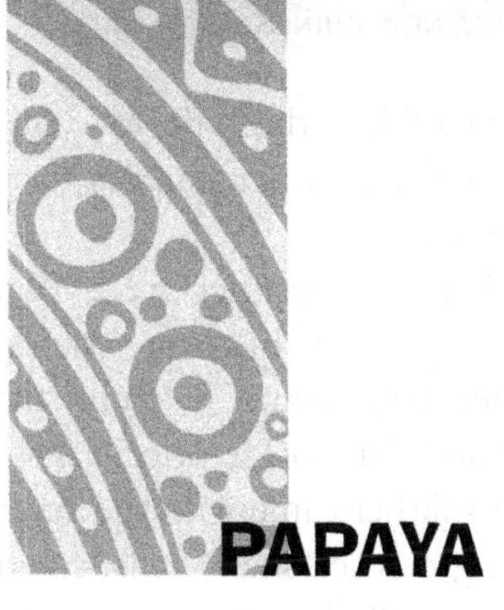

PAPAYA

Amid the steep hills and forested valleys of the Eastern Highlands grows a tree which bears fruit that is soft to the touch, easily bruised, and very sweet to taste. It grows in the wild bush and is cultivated in the village gardens. The children who live in this region know that they must take special care of these trees and their fruit. This story tells how the tree first grew.

Long ago, in the village of Hiwaru, close by the Ramu River, there lived a girl called Papaya. Although she was not beautiful, she had a loving, sweet and gentle nature. The older people of the village knew this and praised Papaya, but the young men looked only at her ill-featured face and thin body, and none of them wanted her as a wife. One by one, all the other girls found husbands, but Papaya remained unmarried. Then, a young man who had recently come to live in Hiwaru with his father decided it was time he found himself a wife. He asked his father if he could find him one, and his father at once thought of the girl with the loving, sweet and gentle nature whom all the elders praised.

'I have heard of just the wife for you, Maning my son,' he said. 'I will go to her parents to ask if you can marry their daughter.'

Papaya's father and mother were very glad when Maning's father asked if his son could marry their daughter, for they had begun to think that she would never find a husband. The bride-price was settled, and the next day Maning's father came with the agreed number of pigs, pearl shells, green sea-snail shells, cowries, and bird-of-paradise feathers, all the precious things which were exchanged for a young girl. And then, according to custom, Papaya was invited to visit the house of Maning and his father.

Word soon spread around the village that Papaya was to marry handsome young Maning. The women gossiped under the Ruga tree as they cooked in its shade, under its branches hung with baskets of food and oven stones, and the string hammocks where the babies slept out of harm's way. The young men gossiped as they sharpened their hunting weapons or helped to tend the village gardens. 'Papaya is to marry Maning!' they told each other. 'Maning's father has paid the bride-price for the only girl in Hiwaru who could not find a husband!'

It wasn't long before Maning discovered that Papaya was indeed the only girl in the village that none of the other young men had wanted to marry. He felt ashamed and knew that the whole village—all the young people, at least—were mocking him for his choice.

'I cannot marry Papaya!' he told his father. 'I do not like her. She will not make me a good wife. I do not want to be her husband.'

Maning's father was very angry and shouted. 'You will

marry Papaya! You will marry her whether you like her or not! Do you think I have unlimited numbers of pigs and shells and feathers to give away?'

And so it was: Maning married Papaya, even though he had come to hate his bride. As for Papaya, what did she feel? She was now the same as the other young women of the village; she had a husband and she wanted to look after him. She hoped that in time he might grow fond of her and give her kind looks instead of scowls. But Maning was not a good husband to gentle Papaya, even after she had borne him two fine sons. He was very strict with her, and would allow her to go to the village gardens only when there was hard work to be done, crops to sow or fruit and vegetables to gather. He forbade her to go at any other time, as the other women did, to gather extra food or simply to enjoy themselves, singing and talking. Often Papaya found that their food was all used up before she was allowed to go to the gardens to get more; this happened so often that their two sons grew thin and weak.

At last even Papaya's gentle and obedient nature rebelled. She made up her mind to go to the gardens to get more food in spite of her husband. But unluckily for her, she chose to visit the very garden where Maning himself had gone to work that day.

When Maning saw his wife and their sons approaching, he was furious. He hid himself in the bush, and watched Papaya carefully. He saw her leave the two boys in the shade of a tree at the edge of the garden, telling Tiro, the eldest, to look after his young brother. Then, she came into the garden and bent down to dig some yams. No sooner had she done so than a spear flew from the bush and took away her right breast. As she screamed, her husband threw a second spear which pierced her head. She fell dying to the ground. Then, her cruel husband came out from his hiding-place, dropped Papaya's body into a pit at the end of the garden, and filled the pit with earth.

Tiro and his brother, meanwhile, had seen nothing of all this.

'Come, children,' Maning said to his sons. 'We are going home now.'

'Where is our mother?' Tiro asked.

'She will come later,' Maning replied.

In the evening, Tiro asked if he might go to meet his mother and help her carry home the yams. But Maning scowled and told him to go to bed.

As Tiro slept, he had a strange dream. His mother appeared before him and told him that no one would ever see her again. She said that he must go to the garden, to the place where she had tried to dig yams. There he would find a small plant growing. He was to look after the plant and see that no harm came to it.

Tiro went to the garden the next morning. There was the plant, just as his mother had described it in his dream, growing in the place where the spears had taken off her breast and pierced her head. Tiro knew that it was a completely strange plant, which no one had ever seen before. He got some sticks and built a little fence around it to protect it, and every day he went to the garden to look after it. The plant grew very fast. In seven days it was higher than the boy himself. After one month, Tiro saw fruit growing on the tree, hard green fruit which after a few more weeks turned yellow.

'Perhaps the fruit is ripe to eat now,' the boy thought. He plucked one: it felt cool and soft. 'What shall I do with this fruit?' he wondered. 'Is it good to eat raw, or should it be cooked?'

As he sat there under the strange tree, suddenly he heard a voice say: 'Eat!' But he could see no one. Again the mysterious voice spoke: 'Eat the fruit, for it is your mother's breast, which gave you nourishment when she was alive.'

Then Tiro looked at the fruit again, and saw that in shape it did indeed resemble the breast of a woman. He broke open its skin. Inside lay soft yellow flesh and a row of shiny seeds. He tasted the flesh; it was delicious, cool and sweet, much sweeter than any fruit he had eaten before.

Tiro picked more of the fruit and took it back to the village. He showed it to his father and gave a piece of it to his brother.

'Be careful!' his father warned as his younger son bit into the soft flesh.

'It will not hurt him; it is our mother's breast, from which she nourished us when she was alive,' Trio told his father.

When Maning heard this, his face turned grey. He made Tiro tell him the exact place where the tree was growing. Then he knew that it had sprung from his wife's breast, after he had speared her.

Meanwhile, all the village had heard of the strange new fruit Tiro had found. Everyone came to taste it, and the oldest man got up and said that it was much sweeter than any other fruit he had ever known in his long life. 'We must give this fruit a name,' he said.

'Let Tiro name the fruit!' the villagers said.

It was not difficult for Tiro to decide what the fruit

should be called. He stood before the whole village and told all the people about the voice he had heard in the garden and the words it had spoken.

'The name of the fruit is Papaya,' he said proudly.

Each village was given a seed of the fruit to plant in the gardens, and that is how the papaya or pawpaw tree came to that place.

PIGS INTO PYTHONS

The pig is highly prized throughout Papua New Guinea: a man reckons his wealth by the number of pigs he owns; so many pigs will make up the price of a bride; and the succulent, sweet-tasting flesh of roasted pig is eaten at ceremonial feasts.

Long ago, when this world was young, a very curious race of pigs flourished in the country around the villages of Bukaua and Wakun, south-east of Lae. They were like no pigs before or since. Not only were they double the size of the pigs that root around the villages today, they were very, very long, so long that when they walked along the ground, they looked like huge snakes on legs. The people believed that when they ate the flesh of these strange pigs, they were protected against all forms of sorcery and evil magic.

Now at that time, a very powerful sorcerer called Tagu lived in this part of the world. Tagu's magic was so strong that people were afraid to live beside him. Tagu knew this, and so he went to live at the very top of a high hill nearby, which was inhabited by a tribe of little people.

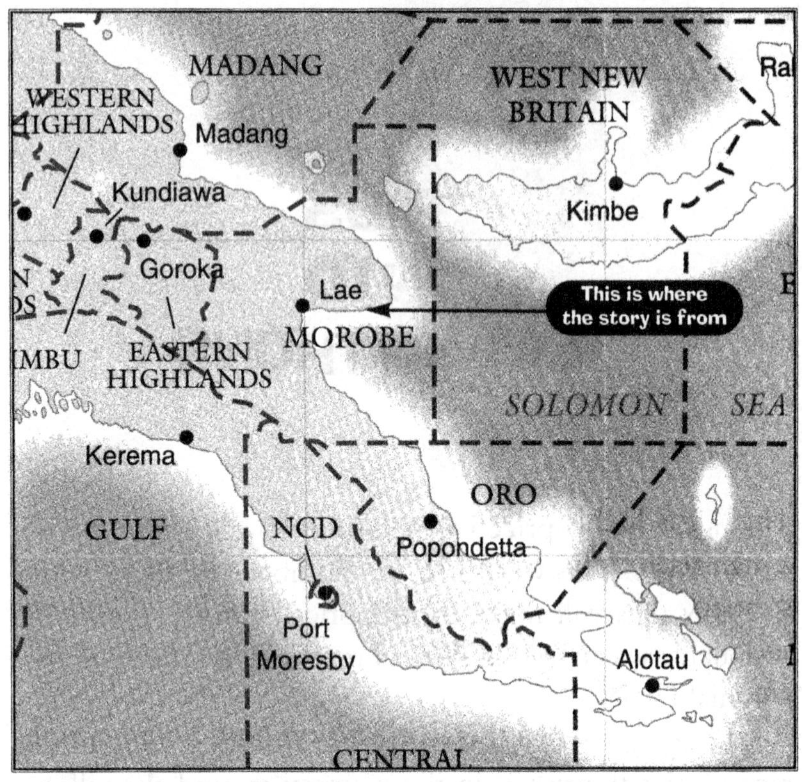

Pigs Into Pythons **was contributed by Jack Nakwa. Jack comes from Bukaua village, east of Lae, in the Morobe Province. He attended Bugandi High School, near Lae, before going on to the University of Technology, Lae, to study surveying.**

These little, dark people were not afraid of Tagu, because they too possessed magic knowledge. Everywhere they went they carried little baskets woven from coconut leaves, which held the secret ingredients they used to make their magic. And because they had the power to weaken any spells or charms that Tagu might make, they had no reason to fear him.

Years beyond number, Tagu lived on that high hill. Often, he would sing his magic chants and send bad magic down to the villagers below; but because the people of Bukaua and Wakun ate the flesh of their pigs, no harm came to them. Tagu often wondered why his magic did not seem to have any effect on the villagers. He guessed they had some secret protection against his spells, and longed to know what it was.

One morning, a man from Wakun Village went fishing in a deep pool beneath a high cliff which was part of the hill where Tagu lived with the pygmy tribe. Imagine the man's astonishment when one of the little dark men came rolling down the hill and landed *splash* in the water. The pygmy, leaning over the top of the cliff to see how the man was catching his fish, had overbalanced and toppled over. He could not swim and floundered about in the water gasping for air, but the fisherman rescued him and took him back to Wakun to recover.

'That's a strange fish you caught today,' the other villagers said. 'Are you going to cook it on the fire and eat it for supper?'

The pygmy shivered with fright when he heard this, but he soon realised the words were spoken with laughter, and that no one intended to harm him.

While the pygmy was in the village, he noticed a few

of the strange pigs that lived there. 'What curious creatures!' he observed.

'Yes,' said the fisherman, 'and they are very valuable creatures, too, for by eating their flesh we protect ourselves from the powerful magic of Tagu the Sorcerer.'

'Tagu lives beside us on the hilltop,' said the pygmy, 'but we do not fear him, for we are able to make our own magic.' Then, he showed the fisherman his little basket containing the secret ingredients for making magic, which he still had with him, even though he had fallen from the cliff and nearly drowned in the deep pool. 'We have the power, not only to turn aside the magic made by others, but also to change humans and creatures into different kinds of animals.'

When the pygmy had recovered from his fall, the fisherman showed him the quickest way back to his hilltop home.

It wasn't long before Tagu heard of the pygmy's adventure. One day, he sought out the pygmy and started up a conversation with him. 'So you have been down to Wakun Village,' he said in a friendly manner. 'Did you see anything remarkable there?'

'Oh yes!' answered the pygmy. 'I saw the strange pigs that live there.' And then, before he realized what he was saying, he added: 'The villagers eat their flesh to turn away evil magic.'

When Tagu learned this, he jumped to his feet in delight. 'At last, I have discovered the secret! Now I know how the villagers have remained unharmed by my magic all these years!' And at once he began to think of a plan to destroy the protection the village people obtained from the pigs' flesh.

'I have it!' he said presently. 'I will turn all the pigs into pythons. The pigs look very much like snakes already—it will not be difficult. The villagers will think that all the pigs have disappeared. They will never think of eating the pythons!'

The pygmy was very sorry that he had told Tagu the villagers' secret, but there was nothing he could do to stop the sorcerer from sending down his bad magic upon Bukaua and Wakun villages. In a little while, all the pigs were changed into huge pythons with forked tongues and sinuous, legless bodies that slithered along the ground. There had never been any pythons in that area before.

The villagers were dismayed when they realized that all the pigs had disappeared. They saw the pythons as they slithered through the grass, but they did not know these were their pigs in a new form. 'We should not have eaten so many of the pigs!' they lamented. 'We have eaten so many that they have not been able to reproduce themselves any more. Aiee! How shall we turn away evil magic now?'

No one could answer this question. That night, however, when all the village was asleep, the fisherman of Wakun woke suddenly to find the pygmy he had rescued standing by his sleeping-place.

'I have come to tell you that Tagu has changed all your pigs into pythons,' the pygmy told him. 'All you have to do to protect yourself against his magic is to eat the flesh of the pythons instead of the pigs.'

Like a shadow he had come and now, like a shadow, he went.

The fisherman of Wakun lost no time in telling the other villagers what had happened, and from that day the people of Wakun and Bukaua began to roast the pythons and eat their flesh instead of the pigs'. And, although Tagu sent down his most powerful spells from the hilltop, no harm came to them.

The sorcerer realised that still his magic had no effect upon the people, and he became more evil-tempered than ever, so that the pygmy people wished he would go away and live somewhere else. Moreover, they had come to realise that the villagers who lived below were friendly people, and they wanted to have more contact with them. So long as Tagu lived on the hilltop, this could never be.

One day, when the sorcerer was sitting on the edge of the cliff, gazing out across the villages and plotting more of his magic, all the pygmies came in a great company and pushed him right over. And as he fell down, down, down below, they uttered a magic spell which changed him into a big chunk of rock. And that was the end of Tagu the Sorcerer, and the beginning of friendship between the little dark men of the hilltop and the villagers of Bukaua and Wakun.

Today, at Bukaua, the big rock which was once Tagu still stands at the bottom of the cliff. And the villagers of Bukaua and Wakun are still eating pythons.

THE WITCHES' FIRE

In the days long ago when men first began to live in the world, they had no fire. Without fire to warm themselves, they shivered through the cold nights; without fire for cooking, they ate their food raw. Gradually a few people discovered how to kindle the warm, leaping flames, and then fire brought a new comfort into their lives. In the area around Bougainville, the first to discover fire were some witches who lived on the tree-clad mountainside. The people who lived down below, in the coastal villages, knew about the witches' fire and longed to share it. But the witches kept the secret of kindling it to themselves, and would not give away any of their fire. Several times the elders of the largest village at the foot of the mountains sent tribesmen to barter for a piece of the witches' fire; always the tribesmen returned empty-handed.

At last, the elders gathered in their meeting-house and decided that they would make one more attempt: they would send a dog to steal a piece of the fire. They called in the most intelligent dog in the village and told him what he was to do. Straight away the dog went into the bush and collected four friends to help him in his task: a

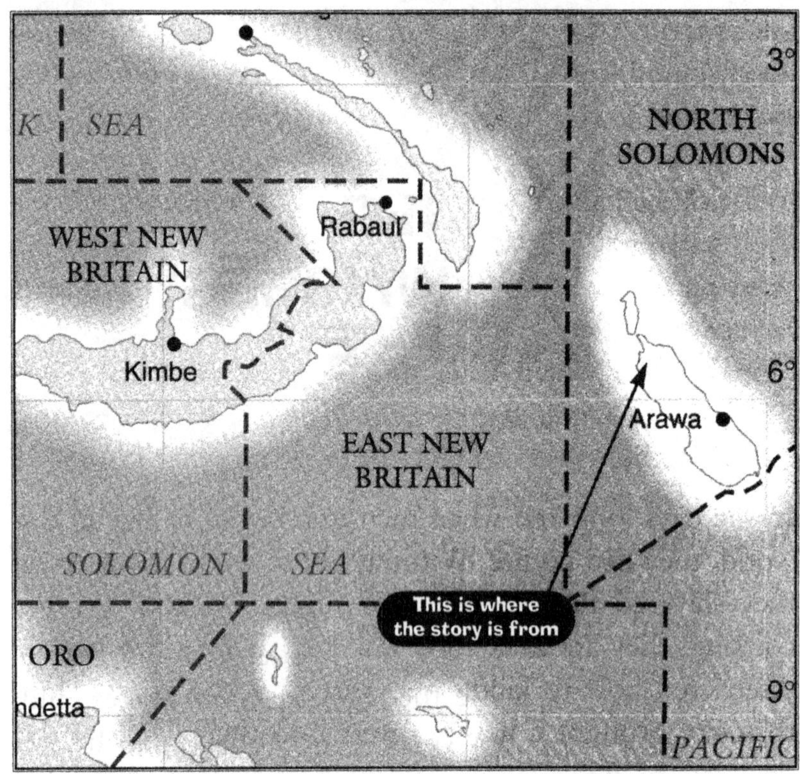

The Witches' Fire **was contributed by Francis Tukan. Francis comes from Saposa village in the Bougainville Province. He attended George Brown High School, near Rabaul, before going on to the University of Technology, Lae, to study mechanical engineering.**

green-feathered parrot; a possum with a long, bushy tail; a long-tailed frog (for in those days all frogs had tails); and a pig. The dog drew up a plan of action. He placed his four friends in different positions along the path that led to the witches' camp. A high kwila tree marked the beginning of the path, and the parrot flew up and perched on one of its branches. Halfway along, the path crossed a river: the possum sat on one bank, and the frog on the other. The pig waited just a short distance from the camp, near the end of the path. Now the dog set off; he swam across the river and followed with his nose the smell of burning wood that came from the witches' fire. When he reached the camp, the witches, wearing bark cloaks, were huddled around their big fire, for it was a cold morning. The flames, orange and red and yellow, leapt upwards.

The witches did not take much notice of the dog; when he asked if he might warm himself by the fire, they made a place for him.

Now as everyone knows, the warmth of a fire can make one feel drowsy and sleepy, and gradually the witches began to doze and snore. The dog watched as one by one their heads nodded and dropped and their eyes closed. Then, he inched his way right to the fire, seized a piece of burning wood in his mouth, and ran off with it.

The witches heard the dog running away; quickly they opened their eyes, saw what he had done, shook off their sleep and began to chase him, shrieking and yelling with rage.

Panting, the dog reached the place on the mountain path where he had left the pig; he gave the piece of burning wood to the pig, who ran on with it until he came to the river. Meanwhile, the dog escaped into the bush, leaving the witches to chase after the pig. On this side of the river the frog sat waiting: the pig tied the piece of burning wood on to the frog's tail—and then the pig, too, escaped into the bush.

The witches threw aside their bark cloaks and jumped into the water, and swam after the frog—but the frog reached the other bank ahead of them. Just as he reached the bank, however, where the possum waited for him, the fire burnt right through his tail, which dropped off: and that is why today, frogs have no tails.

While the frog leapt back into the water and swam away, the possum ran on with the piece of burning wood. The witches scrambled out of the river on to the other bank, pursuing the possum. The possum ran and ran until he reached the tall kwila tree where the green-feathered parrot sat waiting. Just as he scrambled on to the lowest branch of the tree, one of the witches caught up with him and took hold of his long bushy tail. The possum scrambled upward and managed to break free from the witch's grasp. But in doing so, he lost all the hair off his tail, and the witch was left with a handful of fur. And ever since, most possums have had bare, skinny tails.

Now the witches stood under the kwila tree, watching the possum climb up and up until he reached the green parrot who was perched on the topmost branch. He gave the piece of fire to the parrot, who flew away with it in his beak: and when the witches saw that, they realised there was no more they could do, and they gave up the pursuit.

Swiftly the parrot flew over the treetops to the village by the sea from which the dog had set out. As he flew, the fire singed and burnt the green feathers of his breast, so that they glowed red: ever since that time, he has had a red breast.

How gladly the villagers welcomed the parrot when he flew into their midst bearing the precious fire they had wanted for so long! Now they would no longer shiver in the cold; now they could at last cook their food and need no longer eat raw meat. They fetched bundles of dry wood and built a huge fire of their own, and a few days later they made a big feast, to which they invited the dog and his four valiant friends: the parrot, the possum, the frog, and the pig.

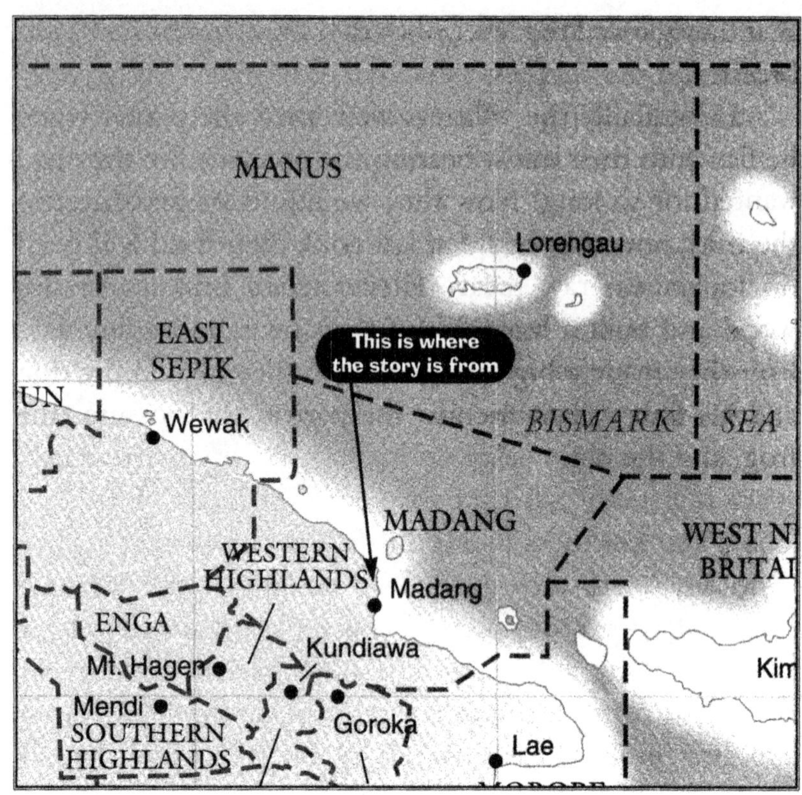

The Snake Bridegroom **was contributed by Otte Karira. Otte comes from Wakorma in the Madang Province. He attended Bumayong Lutheran High School, near Lae, before going on to the University of Technology, Lae, to study accountancy and business studies.**

THE SNAKE BRIDEGROOM

In a village by the sea, north of the place now called Madang, there once lived an old couple who had only one child, a daughter whom they loved dearly. She was a lively, carefree girl and there was nothing in the world she enjoyed so much as fishing. She would go fishing at every possible opportunity. In the daytime, she would fish alone from a large, flat rock surrounded by sea; at night, she would wade into the surf with the other fishermen and women, carrying a sharp spear and a blazing torch. Strings and strings of glittering, glistening fish she would bring home, far more than enough for her mother's cooking fire, and she would give plenty away to the other villagers, who loved her for her generosity.

One morning she got up early, and came outside her father's house to see whether it was a fine day for fishing. The sky was clear, the sea lay sparkling, and the palm-trees along the water's edge seemed to beckon to her as they swayed in a gentle breeze. From the bushland, over the tops of the feathery casuarinas and the tall mu trees, she heard the song of kau, the bird that sings at dawn.

Eagerly, she took out her fishing line and ran to the rock from which she had caught so many fish in days gone past. Her heart sang as she thought of a whole day spent fishing. She cast her line over the water; in a very short time she felt something pull at it. She tried to bring in her catch, but she could not move the line at all. It stayed taut in her hands, and began to pull away from her more and more strongly.

'This must be the grandfather of all fishes I have on the end of my line!' she thought.

She rested a while, then began pulling again; but the outcome of it was that she fell off the rock into the sea, where she was caught by the huge snake that had been snared by her line. Yes, the girl who had caught so many fish in the days gone by was now captured herself!

'Let me go!' she cried, struggling in the water. But the snake held her fast in the coils of his body. 'I shall keep you here until your parents promise that you may be my wife,' he told her.

The girl gazed with horror at the snake. 'I will never marry you!' she said. 'You are ugly and loathsome. I want to marry one of the handsome young men of my village. Let me go!'

But the snake ignored her pleas and held on to her tightly.

In the afternoon, the girl's parents grew anxious when she did not come home at her usual time. They waited and waited, but still she did not come. Then, they walked out of the house and began to look for her in every direction, but there was no sign of her. At last they came to the seashore, where they stood crying and calling for their daughter.

From a troubled patch of sea in the distance they heard a voice answer them. 'If you promise to let me marry your daughter, she will return to you!' It was the voice of the snake. And now they could see the coils of the creature thrashing through the water, and hear their daughter's cries for help.

The poor parents did not know what to do. They certainly did not want their only daughter to become the wife of a snake, yet they thought that if they promised her to him and she was restored to them, they might be able to think of some way to outwit the creature.

So, in a trembling voice, the girl's father promised that she should become the snake's bride. Immediately the snake released the girl, and she was able to swim to the shore.

'In three days I shall come to the village to claim you as my wife!' he hissed as she swam away.

The whole village discussed what had happened; everyone felt sympathy for the poor girl and her parents. The elders of the village met to discuss what should be done, and they made a plan to kill the snake. They prepared a platform where the wedding should take place, but along one side they hid sharpened spears to use against the snake bridegroom.

Three days later, the girl, dressed for her wedding in a new skirt cloth, her skin shining with pandanus oil, her hair decked with scarlet flowers, came to the platform. She walked slowly, her head lowered.

Suddenly the great conch shell at the entrance to the village sounded its deep note—the signal that the snake was approaching. He coiled his way through the trees, across the open space around the village, and past the houses until he came to the platform. His body was painted with ochre and clay, all red and white, and when he saw his bride waiting there for him, he quickened his pace towards her. As he began to mount the platform, the village warriors rushed from one side, where they had been hiding, and killed the snake with their sharp spears. As soon as the people saw he was dead they gave a shout of joy and cut his body into pieces, which they buried alongside the house of the girl's father.

A short while afterwards, the girl was sweeping the ground beside the house when she noticed a small plant growing up from the exact place where the snake had been buried. Then, more plants appeared, as many as the pieces of the snake that lay there; day by day they grew steadily in a clump until they stood as high as a man. No one could tell what sort of a plant this was, for no one had ever seen its like before. Each plant had a hard, round, jointed stalk about the thickness of a man's finger, and sprouted small, slender green leaves. But the most extraordinary feature of the plant was that the stalks were striped red and white.

One day, a village woman left her small son in the girl's charge while she went to the garden. When the boy saw the red-and-white striped plants he began to cry for them. 'Let me have them!' he cried, so many times that at last the girl cut the plant and gave a piece of the stalk to him. He put it in his mouth and began to chew it.

'Try it!' he urged the girl. 'It tastes so sweet and juicy!'

So the girl cut off another piece and tasted it for herself. Yes, it was good—so juicy and so sweet.

It wasn't long before the rest of the village tasted the new plant. They liked it so much that they grew more of it from the seeds of that first clump of plants, and in time other villages began to grow it. Today, sugar-cane grows everywhere in New Guinea. There are different varieties, but still you can see the canes that have red-and-white parallel lines on them, which show how the snake painted himself for the wedding . . . while the juicy part of the cane represents the snake's fat.

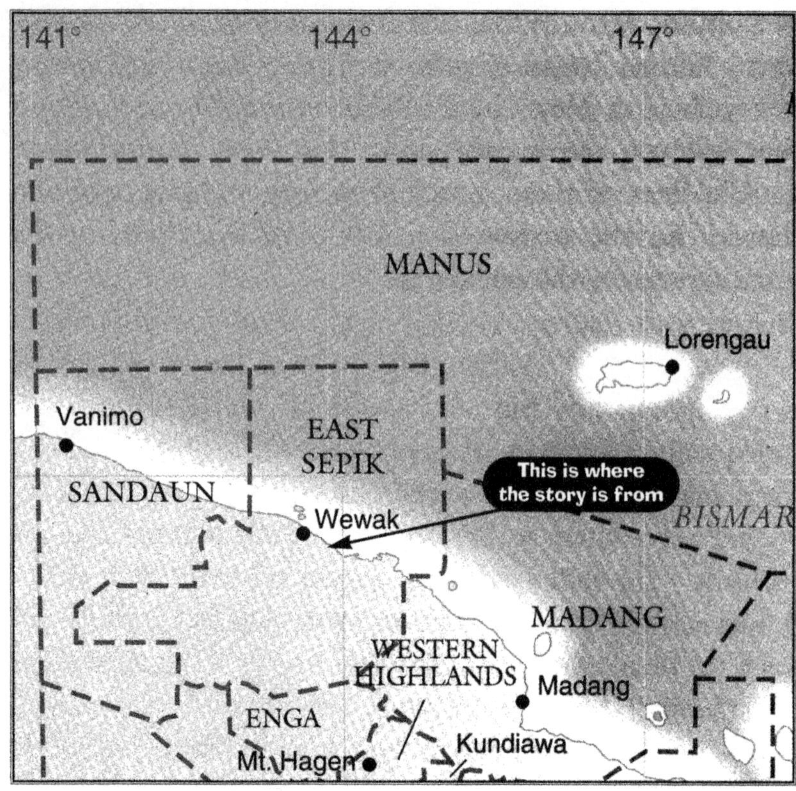

***The Great Flood* was contributed by Adam Amod. Adam comes from Ali Island, near Aitape, in the Sandaun Province. He attended St. Ignatius' High School before going on to the University of Technology, Lae, to study civil engineering.**

THE GREAT FLOOD

In Sandaun Province, a number of small, offshore islands lie beyond the reefs. One of these is Ali Island, which is curiously shaped—narrow at one end and broad at the other. This story, which is often told in the villages of the Province, tells how Ali Island came into existence.

Long, long ago, there was (as there is now) a coastal village called Sumo, west of Aitape. The headman of Sumo had an only son, who fell sick and died. The headman and all the tribespeople were overcome with grief; the hills around the village echoed to the sound of mourning. After the funeral had taken place, the villagers of Sumo, as was the custom, prepared a great feast for all the tribespeople who had mourned the death of the Ayang Natung, the headman's son. Early in the morning on the day of the feast, the young men of the village made ready *Walamil*—the poison rope to catch the fish for the feast. They took the rope to the river, but they could not catch a single fish. While they stood there wondering what they should do, and how all the tribespeople were to be fed, the waters stirred around the poison rope and an enormous eel came to the surface.

'Take away walamil, your poison rope, young men of Sumo,' the eel commanded them. 'This is a bad way to catch fish.'

The young men were angry when they heard the eel speak. They flung their spears at the creature's great coiling body and killed it.

'Now we have nothing to worry about!' they rejoiced. 'The giant eel will provide plenty of food for everyone at the feast!'

Singing, they carried home the eel, and hung it in great loops from a tree branch so that everyone could see it. Then the eel was carved up, and the pieces of flesh divided amongst the villagers, who took them away to cook for the feast. A certain young boy was the last to come for the pieces due to his family; when he had taken his share, all that was left was the eel's head. As the boy was leaving, he was startled to hear a soft voice coming from the head: 'Tell your parents not to eat any of my flesh after it is cooked, when it is handed round at the feast. Instead, take the pieces you have there and bury them under the tall coconut tree that grows at the edge of the village. Your people made a bad mistake when they speared me, for I am the god of the river: my spirit can never die. Tell your father to dig a very large pit beside the coconut tree, where you and your mother may shelter; for I am about to send a great flood upon this village, to destroy all the people. Only you and your family will be saved. While you shelter beneath the ground with your mother, your father can save himself by climbing to the top of the tree until the flood has gone.'

Fearfully the boy told his parents every word the eel had spoken; and while the other tribespeople were enjoying the feast that afternoon, gorging themselves on the eel's tender flesh, laughing and singing amongst themselves while the sun shone in the blue sky, the boy's father, whose name was Kairap, dug a large pit beneath the tall coconut tree, and when he had finished, his wife and son crept into it, and he covered the opening with earth and branches. Then, Kairap himself climbed to the top of the tree and waited for what would happen.

It was not long before the river god's spirit covered the blue sky with black clouds, blotting out the sun. Then, spears of lightning came from the sky, thunder roared around the hills and the rain began. It fell down from the sky in torrents, not only in the village of Sumo, but in all the countryside round about. The river was so swollen that it burst its banks and flooded the land. Still the rain fell from the sky; soon the flood was so great that it swept away whole villages.

One group of tribespeople, who were Yiniy Parey, bushfolk, were still on their way to the feast at Aitape when the rain began; they were crossing the river, using a fallen breadfruit tree as a bridge. They were halfway across when suddenly the swirling river struck the tree, dislodging it and sweeping it downriver towards the sea. They clung to the tree, wondering what their fate would be.

Meanwhile, Kairap sat at the top of the tall coconut tree, watching in wonder as the great flood covered the ground, the houses of the village, and all the smaller trees round about. Countless people and creatures of the bush were drowned. To keep himself alive, Kairap was able to eat the flesh of the coconuts and drink their sweet liquid, while the leaves of the tree gave him shelter.

After some days, he saw that the water was beginning to recede. The trees that had been covered emerged again, and the sad ruins of the village houses, and the bodies of those who had drowned were revealed. He took a coconut and threw it to the around, but it sank out of sight in the earth. This showed that the ground was still too soft to walk upon. Three days later he threw down another coconut; this time when it hit the ground it split open, and Kairap knew it was safe for him to climb down. He was very anxious to see if his wife and son were safe in the underground pit he had dug.

When he stood on the earth once more, he looked around and saw a wisp of smoke curling from a crab-hole in the ground. He knew this smoke must be coming from the cooking-fire in the underground shelter, and he began to dig as fast as he could. Kairap was as happy to find his wife and son safe and well as they were to see him unharmed by the great flood. Joyfully the three of them stood together upon the earth once more. And from that small family, all that was left of the tribespeople of Sumo, sprang all the people who live in that place today.

What of the fate of those tribespeople, the Yiniy Parey, who were carried downriver to the sea on the breadfruit tree? Eastward they travelled over the sea all through the long, dark night, until at last the tree came to a halt. At daybreak they looked about them: they were surrounded by the blue sea, breaking against the rocks of a coral reef, and all around the tree was white coral sand. They had never seen the sea, or a coral reef, or sand before, those people of the bush; they believed the rocks of the reef were the bones of their ancestors, and the harsh sand-grains the teeth of their forefathers. They soon became used to their surroundings, however, and lived by eating the breadfruit from the tree. They saw that the shape of their island was in fact the shape of the breadfruit tree itself: narrow at one end, where the trunk was, and wide at the other, where the branches and leaves spread out. They decided to call the island Ali.

After these people had lived here for a while, new breadfruit plants sprang from the seed of the first fruit, and one day, some of the men swam to a nearby island called Tumleo, where they were able to get fire from the people who lived there, as well as food, cooking pots and housing materials. The Tumleo people were able, too, to offer the men of Ali, young girls who became their wives, and so the population of Ali grew.

That is the story still told today about the origin of the Island of Ali. And there is one strange fact about the people of Ali today: they speak a dialect which is quite different to the speech of the Tumleo islanders, and to that of the people who live on the mainland around Aitape, closest to Ali. Their speech is most like that of the people of Sumo and other villages along the coast westward of Aitape.

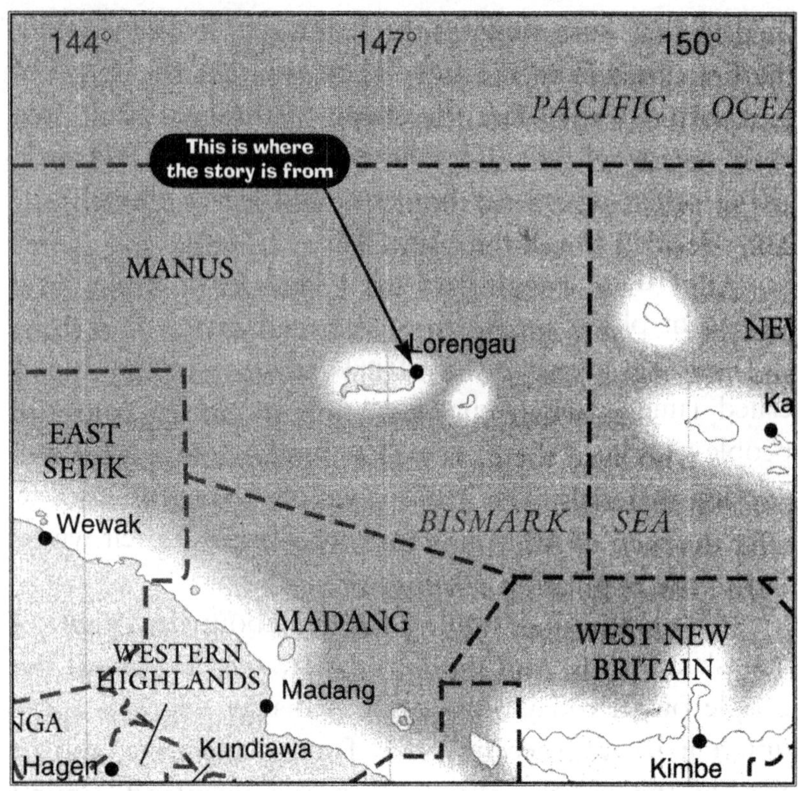

The Woman from The Sea **was contributed by Ivan Ngahan. Ivan comes from Lorengau in the Manus Province. He attended Manus High School, before going on to the University of Technology, Lae, to study electrical engineering.**

THE WOMAN FROM THE SEA

Peheka is a village on Manus Island. Nearby, at a certain place in the rocky coastline, there is a wide, deep hole that goes straight down to the sea. The children of Peheka are warned not to play near this hole in case they should fall into it; the fishermen, too, are careful how they tread on the slippery, sea-wet rocks round about. Not far away, there is a patch of green, sweet-smelling grass; a little farther on, a pool of clear water lies trapped among the rocks.

This is the story the villagers of Peheka tell about the mysterious hole in the rocks, the grassy patch, and the little pool.

Long ago, two sisters called Hinimei and Hinipong lived in that pool of clear water among the rocks. They were not ordinary young women: they were children of the sea, with tails like those of great fishes, covered in shimmering scales. They spent their time swimming and playing in the water, and sunning themselves on the rocks. Although their pool was not very big, it was deep.

One day, Hinimei, the older sister, grew tired of swimming around the pool, diving into its depth and sunning herself on the rocks. She felt restless. 'Let us explore the shore round about this island where we live,' she said to her sister. 'I am tired of staying in this place.'

Hinipong, the younger sister, was happy enough to stay where she was. 'Why should we leave this pool which has always been our home?' she asked.

But Hinimei persuaded her sister to go exploring, and together they leapt into the sea and swam along the shoreline, past white beaches fringed with palm trees and scattered with shells washed up by the sea. For three days they swam, from sunrise to sunset and through the night when the shining moonlight made the sea as bright as day. On the evening of the third day they came to another island off the south coast of Manus. They swam close to a big reef where the sea broke over the rocks in a never-ending line of surf; and suddenly Hinimei felt her long fish-tail caught in the mesh of a widespread net of strong pandanus fibre, set there by a fisherman.

'Help me, sister!' she cried as she struggled to get free. 'Ai-ee! I am caught! I cannot get free!'

But Hinipong, too, was caught in the meshes of the net. The more the two girls struggled, the more entangled they became; at last, exhausted, they lay quietly, resigned to whatever fate should come to them. And by magic arts they changed their appearance so that now they looked just like fish: their women's bodies were covered in shining scales, just like their tails, and their faces and hair became fishlike, too.

In the morning, the fisherman who had set the net in that place—his name was Pakop—came in his canoe to see whether he had caught anything. He took hold of the edge of the net and shook it and pulled it. How heavy it felt!

'Tonight the whole of my village will feast on the fish

I have caught!' he exclaimed.

Then, other men from his village came to help him haul the net ashore. They were astonished to see the two enormous fishes that lay in the net. They took Hinimei and Hinipong into the village, not realising that they were women of the sea.

'Tonight we feast! Tomorrow, too! See the two huge fishes Pakop, the great fisherman, has caught in his net!' they shouted.

Men went out to gather wood that would burn without smoke for the cooking fire, and when it was lit, they prepared a pit, where they baked poor Hinimei, wrapping hot cooking stones in the leaves of the mu tree. But Pakop took Hinipong into his house, and laid fresh taro leaves over her so that she would keep for the next night's feasting.

While the villagers were enjoying the feast, Hinipong, left alone in the house, used her magic knowledge to change herself once more. This time she appeared as a beautiful girl. Gone was her fish-tail; two slender legs took its place. She did not realise what had happened to her sister, and wondered where she was.

Halfway through the feast, Pakop searched for a drinking vessel so that he might drink the soup of the tender, sweet-tasting fish they had eaten; he got to his feet and came to his house to fetch a coconut shell. When he opened the door of the house, Hinipong smelled the sweetness of the baked fish, and knew at once what fate had come to her sister.

'Hinimei! Hinimei!' she shrieked in grief, and began to cry bitterly. 'You have killed my sister,' she told Pakop.

Pakop was very moved by Hinipong's distress; gently he tried to comfort her. He realized now that the two great fishes caught in his net were women of the sea.

'I would never have harmed your sister if I had known who she was,' he told Hinipong.

At once he let the villagers know what had happened, and they stopped their feasting and went inside their houses. The village lay quiet and still.

At last, still with tears springing from her eyes and running down her face like salt sea drops, Hinipong said to Pakop: 'Since you have killed and eaten my sister, there is nothing I can do except stay here and be a wife to you. Tomorrow the south-east wind is due to blow. My home is far away from here; I could not swim through the wild sea during this season, nor could any canoe cross the water.'

Hinipong's words were pleasing to Pakop; not only did he feel sorry for her, but he admired her beauty. 'You may stay here and become a wife to me,' he told her.

A year passed. Hinipong gave birth to a boy, whom she and Pakop named Kamau. The child grew into a strong youth; the thoughts in his head were wise, and he loved to fish and hunt with his father, Pakop. But the other village boys had bad thoughts of Kamau. They were jealous of his hunting skill and his wisdom. One day, as Kamau returned home from fishing in his canoe, he was taunted by the boys as he walked to his father's house.

'Son of a fish-woman!' they jeered. 'Your mother is a fish-woman! Fish-woman! Fish-boy! Fish-boy!' They danced mockingly beside him, making swimming movements with their arms and pretending to gasp for air, as fishes do when they are tumbled from the nets.

Kamau was distressed and told his mother what had happened. At first she told him not to take any notice of the boys' jibes and jeers but the tormenting of Kamau went on and on, day after day; at last he could stand it no longer. Hinipong was sad to see how her son was taunted, and she made up her mind that it was time she took him away from the village.

One morning, she told Kamau to visit a magic woman who lived nearby, and ask her to give him some magic arrows and a bow. Kamau did this. The magic woman did not seem surprised by his request: it was as though she had known he would come. She gave him a small, pliant bow and nine arrows fashioned from razor-sharp bamboo, and asked no questions of him. Meanwhile, Hinipong packed a supply of food and water, and put on her grass skirt. Kamau hid his bow and arrows under his bed, and Hinipong hid her basket of food and water in a corner of the house, so that Pakop would not see these things when he came home that night.

When the kau bird sang at daybreak the next morning, quietly Hinipong woke Kamau. They took the things they had hidden and stole away to the beach. Pakop sighed and stirred in his sleep, but he did not wake.

Hinipong and her son stood at the water's edge, and Hinipong pointed across the sea. Kamau fitted one of the magic arrows to his bow, and as the kau bird sang once more, he shot it in the direction of his mother's pointing finger. With its magic power, the arrow split the sea in two parts, leaving a dry path for them to walk through. So their journey began.

When they reached the place where the first arrow had landed, Kamau shot the next arrow, and again a pathway lay clear before them through the sea. And when Kamau pulled out the first arrow, the waters came together again behind them, so that no one might follow them.

By this time, Pakop had awoken; he was astonished to discover that his wife and son had risen from their sleeping-places. Puzzled at first, then desperate with alarm, he searched for them in vain, and at last went back to his house in sorrow. He knew he would never see his beautiful sea-wife or his son again.

Hinipong and Kamau continued their journey for three days. When darkness fell, the boy made a circle of his arrows all around them, the size of a small house, and here they slept safely. In the morning, they ate some of the food and drank a little of the water Hinipong had brought with her. And all the time they drew nearer to Manus Island, and the place on its rocky coastline where Hinipong and her sister Hinimei had lived so long ago.

At sunset on the third day, Kamau placed his last arrow in the bow and shot it high into the air. It spun round as it fell, and when it reached the shore of the island, it passed right through the rocks, leaving a deep, wide hole that led down, down into the sea. Then, Hinipong and Kamau climbed out of the seabed, right up through that hole in the rocks, and came at last on to the dry land. And when Kamau pulled out that last arrow, the sea once more surged about the rocks, but the hole remained.

They rested under a palm-tree, and Hinipong threw away her grass skirt. Now they had only a short distance to travel, for they were very near the end of their journey. In a little while they came at last to the pool among the rocks where once Hinnipong had lived with her sister Hinimei.

'This is our home,' Hinipong told Kamau happily.

And here they lived for the rest of their lives.

Today, the villagers of Peheka point to the patch of green, sweet-smelling grass which grew from the skirt that Hinipong threw away, and to the big hole in the rocks from which she and Kamau emerged on to the land. And the pool still lies among the rocks, clear and blue and very deep.

THE DRUMS OF TIMPENNI

The drums of Papua New Guinea, made from hollowed-out logs both large and small, covered at either end with the tightly stretched skin of lizards or goannas, are used for many purposes: their voices speak over the distance to send messages, to celebrate tribal rites, to proclaim war. And some, like the great drums of Timpenni, have been known to hold an evil power in their throbbing sound.

Timpenni is a small offshore island southeast of Port Moresby; in days gone by it was an island famous for its magic drums. It is said that their magic was so powerful that it could draw young people from the mainland into the sea, even those who could not swim. Those who did swim over to Timpenni were sold into slavery by the folk who lived on the island.

The Magani, the mainland people who lived in the villages closest to Timpenni, shivered when they heard the relentless, insistent throb of those evil drums, and at last the day came when the village elders decided to attack the island and overcome its bad magic for all time.

The attack took place. Swiftly, the war canoes of the Magani sped across the water, and because they had taken

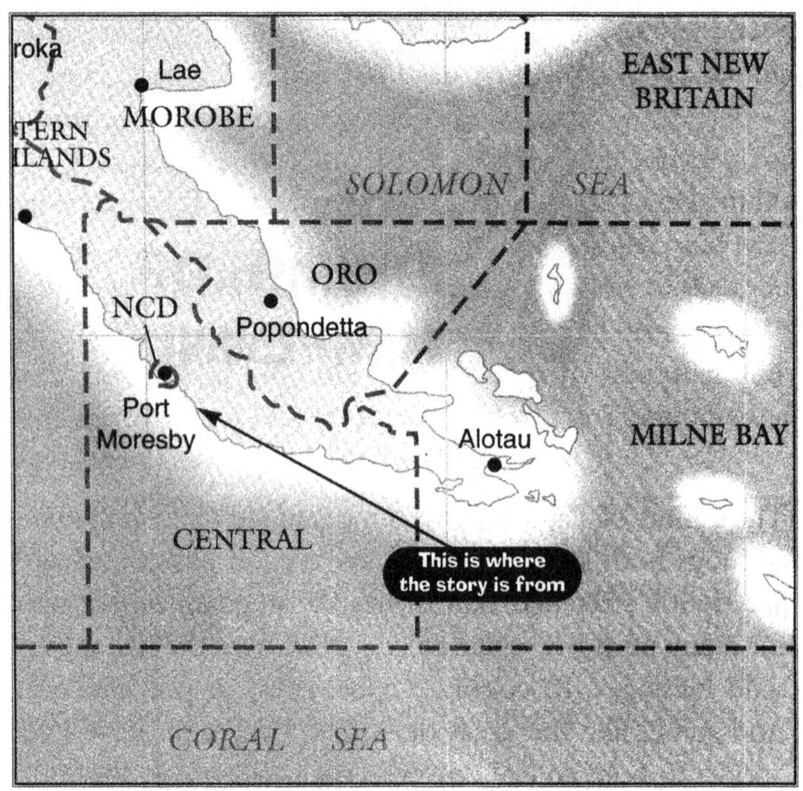

The Drums Of Timpenni **was contributed by Manoka Nou. Manoka comes from Kapa Kapa village in the Central Province. He attended Kwikila High School, before going on to the University of Technology, Lae.**

the Timpenni tribesmen by surprise, the mainlanders succeeded in overwhelming them. They seized all the drums they could find, as well as the men who played them, and destroyed both drums and men. But there was one drum they did not find, nor did they find its drummer or his son. And when the Magani returned home, singing and shouting their victory, that man hid himself in a cave with his son and his drum. He blocked the cave mouth with stones so that no sound should escape, and over the next few years he taught his son the evil art of the great drums of Timpenni.

In time the drummer died, and then the son, who was now a youth, travelled to the mainland with his magic drum. He was determined to seek vengeance for the Maganis' slaughter of the Timpenni tribespeople. As he journeyed, he used the drum to help him on his way. Once, at the edge of the forest, a large wild cat crossed his path and seemed about to leap upon him. The youth began to beat the drum: softly it throbbed with an almost purring sound, and the wild cat began to roll on the ground like a kitten, and finally fell asleep.

Eventually, the young drummer arrived at a village called Knagalu, where the people made fun of him, laughing at him and scorning him. He was so angry at this treatment that he decided to use the Knagalu people to obtain the vengeance he desired upon the Maganis. He began to beat his drum so that it sounded mournfully, such a gentle sound to begin with that the Knagalu people found themselves strangely touched by its sad beat. Gradually the drumbeats quickened, however, and grew louder: and now the drum sounded a roar of hate, and as they listened the people began to feel fierce and warlike, to stamp the ground with their feet, to shake their spears and shout aloud. At the height of their frenzy, while the drum still throbbed, the youth stood up and told the Knagalu to go out and avenge his father's slaughtered kinsmen, to attack the Magani people in their jungle village. As though they had no will of their own, but must obey the drummer and his drum, the Knagalu went forth to the attack, even though it was to avenge no quarrel of their own.

The Maganis were good fighters, and once they had recovered from the first surprise of the Knagalus' attack, they resisted them strongly, and killed many of them, so that the Knagalu warriors began to retreat. When the young drummer saw how the fight was going, he changed the drumbeat so that now the drum called to the Magani to lure them into the jungle, and they grew reckless and careless, chasing the Knagalu warriors far into the forest. And now the Knagalu turned and regrouped themselves, then attacked the Magani afresh and killed nearly all of them.

The chief of all the villages round about, when he heard of this battle, was very angry. He decided to set out alone to find the drummer and kill him, and destroy the evil drum. The chief was a cunning warrior, so skilled in jungle lore that he could creep upon an enemy, be it man or beast, without a sound. He tracked the drummer and leapt upon him before the youth had time to beat his drum to protect himself. The chief speared him and burned the drum, and then he ordered the Knagalu to pay the Magani for what they had done to them. And after the death of the last of the Timpenni drummers and the destruction of that last remaining drum with its evil magic, all the villagers lived peacefully together.

THE GIFT OF THE WHITE COCKATOO

A long time ago, when the world was young and new, there were still some people who had not discovered the existence of fire. They used to shiver when the weather grew cold, and all the food they ate was raw and uncooked. They had no fires in their villages where they could sit and gossip and tell stories; in the hours of darkness, only the moon gave them light.

In one such village, close by the sea, there lived a beautiful girl called Dawe. The young men of the village had eyes only for her. They looked with admiration and desire upon her smooth, dark skin and shining eyes, and ignored all the other girls. This made the other women jealous, so jealous that they plotted to get rid of Dawe. 'Then the young men will look at us instead!' they told each other. 'They will see that we, too, are young and comely!'

Every year, at a certain time, all the young women used to paddle their canoes across the sea to the island that stood farthest away from the mainland. This was the season for gathering seashells, which the villagers used for different purposes: as eating and drinking vessels and for

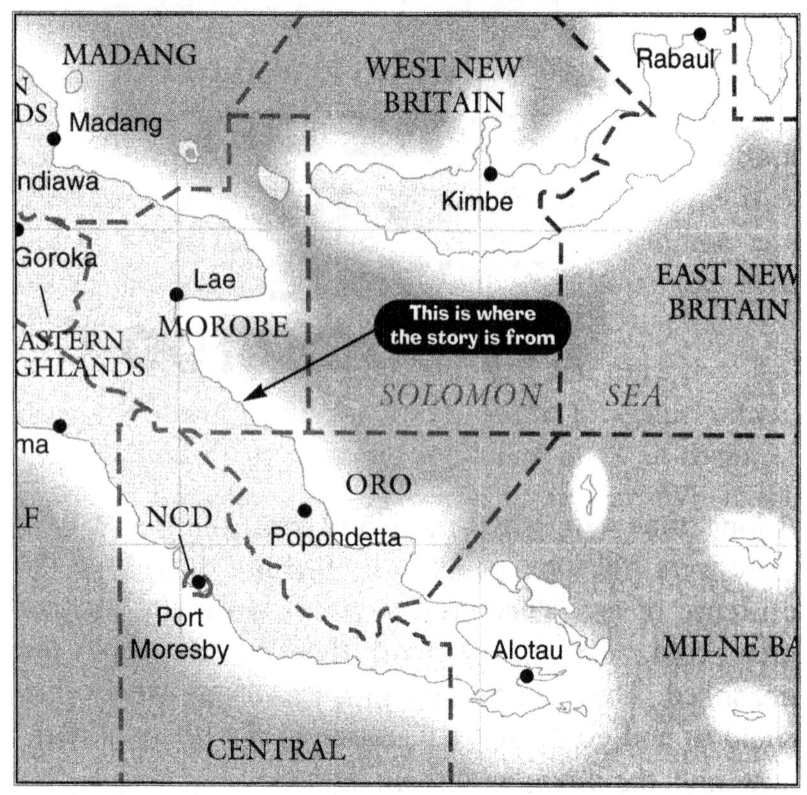

The Gift Of The Cockatoo **was contributed by Kwalam Apisah. Kwalam comes from Buso village in the Morobe Province. He attended Bugandi High School, near Lae, before going on to the University of Technology, Lae, to study surveying.**

decoration. The most rare and valuable shells of all they used as money. The price of a bride could be calculated in shell money, and a sorcerer would accept a certain amount of shells to make a spell or avert evil. Happy the man who wore many precious shells around his neck at the dancing ceremonies!

As soon as the young women beached their canoes upon the shore of the islands this year, they scattered to pick up all the shells they could find, placing them carefully in the bilums, the string bags they had brought with them. A few of the most precious shells were to be found at the bottom of the sea, and some of the girls dived through the gently rolling surf to fetch them up.

Dawe felt tired after the long journey from the mainland. When she had drawn up her canoe on to the sand, she lay down under a palm-tree to rest. The hot sun made her drowsy, and soon she was fast asleep. As soon as the other girls saw she was asleep, they quietly got into their canoes and paddled away, taking Dawe's canoe with them. They had planned to do this before they left the village; by going to sleep, Dawe had made it easier for them to carry out their plan. Halfway between the island and the mainland, the women sank Dawe's canoe, then paddled back to the village happy in the thought that now, without Dawe, the young men would look at them with admiration and desire.

Beneath the swaying palm-tree on the island, Dawe still slept. Suddenly a coconut husk fell upon her; she woke with a start. She looked around. How quiet it was! She could not hear any laughter or chattering—there was no sign of her companions. She went to the place where she had left her canoe and saw that it had gone, along with all the others. She saw all the footprints leading into the water, and knew then that the other girls had deserted her.

She began to weep, but above the sound of her weeping she heard a voice calling to her from the palm-tree. She looked up and saw a white cockatoo.

'Your companions have left you alone on the island because they were jealous of you,' the cockatoo told her. 'They have gone back to the village, where they will say that your canoe overturned and sank, and that you were drowned. So no one will come to look for you.'

When Dawe heard this, she wept more bitterly than before, but the cockatoo told her to dry her tears. He promised to look after her until her people returned to the island in a year's time, when the shell-collecting season came round again.

'Will you fetch food for me?' Dawe asked.

The cockatoo nodded his handsome, crested head, and Dawe told him to fly to the village and bring all the taro that was growing in her garden. So the cockatoo flew back and forth across the sea many times until he had brought every plant from the garden.

'Now we can eat,' Dawe said, and she took up some of the raw taro and offered it to the cockatoo.

'What!' he exclaimed. 'Do you eat taro like that? Raw? You should cook it first!'

'Cook?' asked Dawe, puzzled. 'What is that? My people always eat their food just as they find it.'

Then, the cockatoo took two dry sticks and began to twirl them around each other, so that they rubbed together. In a little while a spiral of smoke appeared, and finally they burst into flame. When Dawe saw fire for the first time, she leapt back in alarm.

'What is that heat you have made?' she asked fearfully. 'Are you a magician? Have you stolen the sun?'

The cockatoo told her not to be afraid. 'This heat is called fire,' he said. 'More and more people are learning its use. When men have fire, they no longer feel cold; they are able to make light in the darkness; and they can cook their food.'

He showed Dawe how to cook the taro on the fire, and when it was ready, they ate it together.

'How sweet and good the taro tastes when it is cooked!' Dawe exclaimed. 'How I wish I could show all the people of my village this fire, so that they too could cook their food, and make warmth and light!'

A year went by. Dawe made a new garden on the island, and lived there happily with the white cockatoo. Sometimes, however, she thought sadly of the family she had left behind in the village, of her father and mother, her brothers and sisters. And now the season for collecting shells came round again, and once more the young girls of the village prepared to come to the island. By this time, everyone believed that Dawe had died, even the girls themselves; they did not think she could have survived alone on the island. Many of them had become wives during the year, and they no longer felt neglected and unhappy.

'This time we will go with you to the island,' the young men said. 'No other girl must drown as Dawe did. We will make sure this does not happen.' And when they spoke Dawe's name, their eyes were sad as they recalled her beauty.

Imagine everyone's astonishment when they got to the island and saw Dawe standing on the shore, waiting to greet them.

'What happened? How is it you are still alive? We thought you had drowned!' the young men exclaimed.

The young women were silent and fearful, but Dawe did not reveal how they had deserted her, for she did not want the men to turn against their wives.

When the young men and women saw the fire Dawe had made on the island, they drew back fearfully, just as Dawe herself had done when she first saw the bright flames.

'Is this truly Dawe, or is it her ghost?' they muttered. 'Surely this is strong magic.'

Dawe told them how the cockatoo had revealed the secret of fire to her, and taught her how useful it was. And when they all went back to the village, they lit the first fire there, and began to cook their food, to warm themselves, and to lighten the darkness with torches. And always after that they made sure that their fire never went out.

Dawe's family were proud that their daughter had shown the people the use of fire. Gladly they agreed that she might become the wife of the white cockatoo, and their marriage feast was celebrated with glad rejoicing.

Printed in Australia
19 Oct 2018
687756

9 780195 540772